Business Letters

SIMPLIFIED AND SELF - TAUGHT

WILLIAM M. FARBER

ARCO PUBLISHING, INC.
NEW YORK

To Barbara, for all the understanding and assistance she provided during the creation of this guide.

Published by Arco Publishing, Inc.
215 Park Avenue South, New York, N.Y. 10003

Library of Congress Cataloging in Publication Data

Farber, William M.
  Business letters, simplified and self-taught.

  Includes index.
  1. Commercial correspondence—Handbooks, manuals,
etc. I. Title.
HF5726.F37   651.7′5   82-3890
ISBN 0-668-05554-5 (Reference Text)   AACR2
ISBN 0-668-05394-1 (Paper Edition)

Printed in the United States of America

CONTENTS

INTRODUCTION

Effective business-letter writing is the concern of virtually everyone in today's business community. Secretaries, administrative assistants, and office managers are just some of the people who must be able to produce a business letter that reflects a positive image of the writer and the organization. This concise, easy-to-follow, letter-writing handbook will make you an expert in writing the kind of correspondence that speaks well of you and your company.

Business Letters Simplified and Self-Taught is really two books in one. It is a style book that guides you through the mechanics of business correspondence and a collection of model business letters for different occasions and formats. It contains step-by-step instructions, diagrams, and examples to help you refine your correspondence skills and produce perfect business letters. Facsimiles of Block letters, Hanging-Indent letters, and Half-Sheet letters are included, as well as other formats for business correspondence.

The many illustrations of layout, spacing, and style are supplemented by a handbook of mechanics and lists of trite expressions to avoid. Besides being able to transcribe your notes into a correct, professional-looking letter, you will now be able to compose a clear, articulate letter from a mere outline. You will welcome letter-writing rather than fear it.

This book will help you communicate efficiently in the current, less formal style that is favored by today's executives.

1
CONTEMPORARY BUSINESS WRITING STYLE

In business, a letter or memo is often the only contact people have with one another. This means that business people are personally represented by the style of their correspondence, whether writing a request, a reply, or a complaint. When it is necessary to communicate on paper, it is important to leave a positive, clear impression with the reader. Remember these six rules:

1. Be neat
2. Be direct
3. Be polite
4. Be personal
5. Avoid sexism
6. Avoid clichés

Business writing that follows these basic rules will send effective messages *and* images to readers.

Above all, the most important factors in business correspondence are a clear plan for your writing and devotion to high-quality results. This book will serve as an effective guide to developing an essential style of letter and memo production; but be sure to follow all directions. Plan ahead. Determine just what your letter has to say and limit it to only those things. Use the Simplified Letter Planner in Chapter 7. Effective messages come from simple correspondence. Keep the six basic rules in mind whenever you write letters. Following these rules will quickly and easily shape your business correspondence into a public-relations image booster.

1.1 NEAT PRESENTATION

First impressions left by your business correspondence are extraordinarily important: the quality of your presentation sets that initial and lasting tone for readers. Care and pride in writing and typing business correspondence takes little extra time but pays great dividends in conveying a positive personal image. After all, if the style of your business correspondence illustrates a lack of interest or pride in high quality, can you expect readers to believe your claims of excellence for your services or products? As a means of first contact between businesses and people, the business letter indicates organizational style, no matter what the size of the firm. In order to leave a lasting and positive first impression, keep in mind these simple steps for creating attractive and useful letters:

1. Use high-quality stationery which has good erasing or correcting qualities. Use correct envelopes.

2. Choose a modern letter style (such as Full Block, Block, Simplified, Modified Semi-Block, or Hanging-Indent letter) detailed in the chapter on letter styles. Follow exactly the rules for construction of these letters.

3. Place the letter correctly on the page. The design and balance of a letter is the first quality apparent to readers.

4. Punctuate correctly. Select a method of punctuation appropriate for the letter style and be sure to follow it consistently throughout the letter.

5. Typing should be accurate and neat. Erasures and corrections should be invisible in finished letters.

1.2   DIRECT DISCUSSION

Letters are intended to transmit messages from the writer to the reader. Only rarely does a discussion of the weather, restaurants, or good books to read fit into business correspondence. Nothing is more discouraging during a busy day at work than wading through extraneous material in order to find out what a writer wants to say. Do not forget that letters are read by people; common courtesies are important. But in business, time is money; so put your reader's time to good use when writing a letter by sticking to these guidelines:

1. State clearly and exactly what is wanted. Every written letter has a purpose. Be sure your reader knows precisely what your purpose is.

2. State the reason or reasons for the inquiry, if at all practical. In business, people will be more likely to oblige requests if they know not only *what* is wanted, but also *why* it is wanted.

3. Logically order the ideas in your letter. Readers must understand the reasoning behind what is discussed. Making readers understand the ideas in your letter is your responsibility.

4. Make sure that all data and statistics in your letters are correct. Even the best letters can be ruined by inaccurate numbers or charts. Check all facts before writing the letter, and check again before signing and sending the letter.

5. Make sure that the language used in the letter is clear and grammatically correct. Trim what is written so that it states exactly, and only, what needs to be said. Do not add useless, space-filling words.

1.3   COURTESY TOWARD READERS

Good business letters have to be read to have their desired effect. The reader will not consider what a letter says if it addresses him or her in a manner that is brusque or discourteous. Keep in mind how your reader will feel when he or she reads your letter. Each reader has a different perspective, and may react badly not only to what you say, but to how you say it. Consider these ideas:

1. Orient your writing toward your reader. Even in letters of complaint, stress your appreciation for the reader's services or products. Make it clear that you value the time your reader spends inspecting correspondence and satisfying requests for help or information.

2. Target your writing toward the reader's expertise. Determine whether lengthy explanations of facts are necessary; they may be inappropriate when writing to specialists in certain fields. If you are discussing something unique or obscure, be sure to explain the facts fully.

3. Use polite expressions. For every occasion, there is a discreet and courteous way to say what has to be said. Being considerate does not have to mean fawning over readers.

1.4 PERSONALIZED COMMUNICATION

Although courtesy goes far in writing effective letters, it is possible to produce a letter that is polite but impersonal. Despite the presence of large firms in today's business community, all letters are read by individuals. Involve your readers in your business correspondence by remembering the following:

1. In the modern business-letter style, readers can be referred to with the personal pronoun *you*. In all business correspondence there is one intended reader toward whom any letter is directed. Address him or her personally and specifically throughout all correspondence.

2. Minimize, but do not totally avoid references to *I* or *we*. Be aware that it is possible to write a letter to a person without making it clear that the letter is also from an individual. Emphasize the *you* (reader) attitude in your letters, but at the same time avoid depersonalization of *I* (writer) in business correspondence.

1.5 NONSEXIST WRITING

Contemporary business correspondence has to be sensitive to changing social and economic trends. Knowledge of the changing roles of both men and women in the workplace is of prime importance. It is becoming more and more likely that business letters will be read by executives concerned with sexual equality in the business community. The concept of modern, nonsexist business writing can be put into effective use by adherence to these basic ideas:

1. Both men and women own, manage, and work in firms throughout the commercial world. When writing a business letter or a memo, make it clear that you know about and appreciate the contributions of both sexes in delivering a service or product.

2. Old, traditional ways of referring to men and women in the work force have become outdated, if not actually rude. The "men" or "women" referred to unconsciously in business correspondence should be replaced with terms that are not sex-

identified. It is not merely fashionable to refer to "businesspeople" instead of "businessmen" or "chairperson" instead of "chairman"; it is both courteous and practical. Business correspondence showing respect toward readers of both sexes will in turn elicit respect for you, the writer.

1.6 FREEDOM FROM CLICHÉS

Paralleling the ideas and methods of direct, precise communication, the avoidance of clichés seeks to trim business correspondence of verbal excess and focus its message. Certain common and familiar expressions simply have no place in a modern writing style. These patterns of speech are overused, outdated, and sometimes redundant. (See Chapter 8 for a review of clichés and unnecessarily long wordings.) There are simpler, shorter, and more distinct ways to express traditional ideas:

1. Avoid stilted constructions for common and frequently used expressions. Adopt more natural ways to say things; often these ways are shorter and will get your messages across more clearly.

2. Trite and overused expressions most often occur at the beginning or the end of a letter, making the expressions most visible. Consult the list entitled "Terms and Expressions to Avoid" in section 8.11. Use suggested alternatives to the older, overworked expressions, or adapt them to fit your personal writing style.

2

MODERN LETTER STYLES

Modern business correspondence has assumed several formats as acceptable styles. Each of these formats has its own individual characteristics and a preferred punctuation pattern. Frequently, companies will adopt a certain style as a matter of general policy; this makes certain letters from that firm easily recognizable. At the present, these forms of letter style are in popular use:

1. Simplified letter
2. Full Block letter
3. Block letter
4. Modified Semi-Block letter
5. Hanging-Indent letter
6. Indented letter

For most business correspondence, the use of any one of these forms will be appropriate.

2.1 SIMPLIFIED LETTER

Recently, administrators and managers concerned with office efficiency have paid considerable attention to reducing the time taken up in typing correspondence. The Simplified letter is the result of their efforts. Because it has fewer and less complex internal parts, the Simplified letter is gaining popularity as the letter format of choice in many businesses.

Special Features of the Simplified Letter

1. All lines begin at the left margin. Paragraphs are not indented.
2. The salutation and the complimentary closing are omitted.
3. The subject line, which serves to summarize the message, is used. It is flush with the left margin, beneath the inside address. It is completely capitalized and unheaded. (See section 4.7.)
4. First and last sentences of the message are often used to convey greetings and regards to the reader.

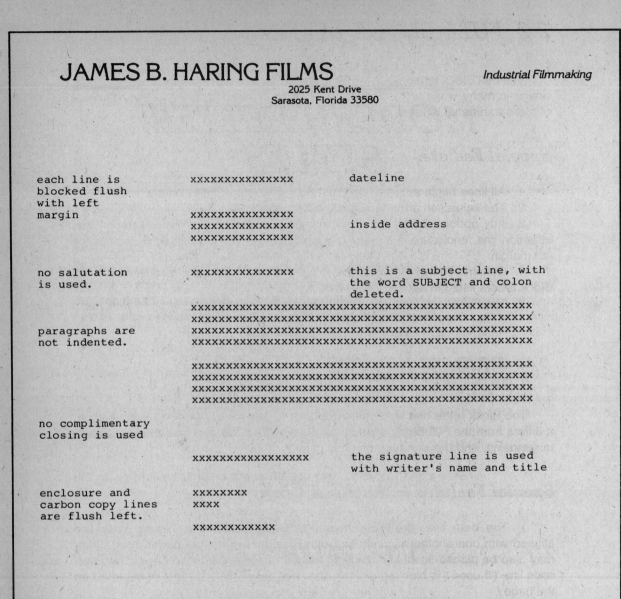

ILLUSTRATION 1. SIMPLIFIED LETTER

5. The signature block should follow the construction recommended for the Simplified letter in section 4.9.

6. The open punctuation style is the only punctuation type used in the Simplified letter. This combination of format and punctuation offers the highest efficiency in producing modern business letters.

2.2 FULL BLOCK LETTER

The Full Block letter rivals the Simplified letter in ease of construction. Although similar in many ways to the Simplified letter, this very popular style offers the use of more traditional letter parts.

Special Features of the Full Block Letter

1. All lines begin at the left margin. Paragraphs are not indented.
2. The salutation and the complimentary closing are used.
3. Any optional letter part or parts may be used (subject line, reference line, attention line, enclosure lines, etc.); if included, the part is blocked flush with the left margin.
4. Construction of individual letter parts should follow the guidelines for Full Block letters listed in sections 4.1–4.14.
5. The Full Block letter uses either the open or the mixed punctuation style.

2.3 BLOCK LETTER

The Block letter has long been a popular format for business correspondence. It differs from the Full Block letter in the placement of the date line, the complimentary closing, and the signature block.

Special Features of the Block Letter

1. The date line, the complimentary closing, and the signature block are aligned with one another, usually beginning five spaces right of page center. They may also be placed flush with the right margin or centered on the page. The reference line (if used) is blocked directly above or below the date line, or centered on the page.
2. All other letter parts are blocked flush with the left margin.
3. Any optional letter part (or parts) may be used; if included, the part is blocked flush with the left margin.
4. Construction of individual letter parts should follow the guidelines for Block letters listed in sections 4.1–4.14.
5. The Block letter uses either the open or the mixed punctuation style.

2.4 MODIFIED SEMI-BLOCK LETTER

The Modified Semi-Block letter is a somewhat more conservative variation of the Block letter style. Since it requires indentation of first paragraph lines throughout the message and indentation of the postscript, typing letters of this style is not quite as simple as typing the non-indented letter formats.

NEWTOWN CONSTRUCTION COMPANY *SINCE 1955*

445 OAK STREET
WESTON, CONNECTICUT 06880

```
each line is           xxxxxxxxxxxxxx          dateline
blocked flush with
left margin
                       xxxxxxxxxxxxxx
                       xxxxxxxxxxxxxx          inside address
                       xxxxxxxxxxxxxx

all special            xxxxxxxxxxxxxxxxxxx     salutation
notations, if used,
are flush with left
margin                 xxxxxxxxxxxxxxxxxxx     subject line (optional)


                       xxxxxxxxxxxxxxxxxxxxxxxxxxxxxxxxxxxxxxxxx
                       xxxxxxxxxxxxxxxxxxxxxxxxxxxxxxxxxxxxxxxxx
                       xxxxxxxxxxxxxxxxxxxxxxxxxxxxxxxxxxxxxxxxx
paragraphs are
not indented           xxxxxxxxxxxxxxxxxxxxxxxxxxxxxxxxxxxxxxxxx
                       xxxxxxxxxxxxxxxxxxxxxxxxxxxxxxxxxxxxxxxxx
                       xxxxxxxxxxxxxxxxxxxxxxxxxxxxxxxxxxxxxxxxx
                       xxxxxxxxxxxxxxxxxxxxxxxxxxxxxxxxxxxxxxxxx


                       xxxxxxxxxxxxxxxx        complimentary closing



                       xxxxxxxxxxxxxxxx        signature line(s)

enclosure and          xxxxx
carbon copy lines      xxxx
are flush left
                       xxxxxxxxxx
```

ILLUSTRATION 2. FULL BLOCK LETTER

8

Alabama Paper Incorporated

45 SOUTHERN PARKWAY
MOBILE, ALABAMA 36607

dateline   xxxxxxxxxxxxxxxxxxx

                         xxxxxxxxxxxxxx
each line is blocked   xxxxxxxxxxxxxx   inside address
flush with the   xxxxxxxxxxxxxx
left margin

                         xxxxxxxxxxxxxx   salutation

                         xxxxxxxxxxxxxxxxxx   subject line (optional)

                         xxxxxxxxxxxxxxxxxxxxxxxxxxxxxxxxxxxxxxxxxxxxxxx
paragraphs are   xxxxxxxxxxxxxxxxxxxxxxxxxxxxxxxxxxxxxxxxxxxxxxx
not indented   xxxxxxxxxxxxxxxxxxxxxxxxxxxxxxxxxxxxxxxxxxxxxxx

                         xxxxxxxxxxxxxxxxxxxxxxxxxxxxxxxxxxxxxxxxxxxxxxx
                         xxxxxxxxxxxxxxxxxxxxxxxxxxxxxxxxxxxxxxxxxxxxxxx
                         xxxxxxxxxxxxxxxxxxxxxxxxxxxxxxxxxxxxxxxxxxxxxxx
                         xxxxxxxxxxxxxxxxxxxxxxxxxxxxxxxxxxxxxxxxxxxxxxx

                         complimentary   xxxxxxxxxxxxxxxxxxxxx
                           closing

                         signature line(s)   xxxxxxxxxxxxxxxxxxxxx

enclosure and   xxxxxxxxx
carbon copy lines   xxxxx
are flush left
                         xxxxxxxxxxx

ILLUSTRATION 3. BLOCK LETTER

BETTS TAPE COMPANY
344 Commerce Drive
Pittsburgh, Pennsylvania 15219

                                    dateline   xxxxxxxxxxxxxxxxxxxx

each line is blocked   xxxxxxxxxxxxxxxx
flush with the   xxxxxxxxxxxxxxxx   inside address
left margin   xxxxxxxxxxxxxxxx

                       xxxxxxxxxxxxxxxx   salutation

subject line (optional)   xxxxxxxxxxxxxxxxxxxxxxxx
  centered on page

                            xxxxxxxxxxxxxxxxxxxxxxxxxxxxxxxxxxxxxxxx
                       xxxxxxxxxxxxxxxxxxxxxxxxxxxxxxxxxxxxxxxxxxxxx
first line of each   xxxxxxxxxxxxxxxxxxxxxxxxxxxxxxxxxxxxxxxxxxxxx
paragraph is   xxxxxxxxxxxxxxxxxxxxxxxxxxxxxxxxxxxxxxxxxxxxx
indented
                            xxxxxxxxxxxxxxxxxxxxxxxxxxxxxxxxxxxxxxxx
                       xxxxxxxxxxxxxxxxxxxxxxxxxxxxxxxxxxxxxxxxxxxxx
                       xxxxxxxxxxxxxxxxxxxxxxxxxxxxxxxxxxxxxxxxxxxxx
                       xxxxxxxxxxxxxxxxxxxxxxxxxxxxxxxxxxxxxxxxxxxxx

                       complimentary   xxxxxxxxxxxxxxxxxx
                          closing

                       signature line(s)   xxxxxxxxxxxxxxxxxx

enclosure and   xxxxxxxxxx
carbon copy lines   xxxxx
are flush left
                       xxxxxxxxxxxx

ILLUSTRATION 4. MODIFIED SEMI-BLOCK LETTER

Special Features of the Modified Semi-Block Letter

1. The date line, the complimentary closing, and the signature block are aligned with one another, usually beginning five spaces right of page center. They may also be placed with the longest line of these letter parts flush with the right margin. The reference line, if used, is blocked directly above or below the date line, or centered on the page.

2. The first line of each paragraph and the postscript (if used) are indented five spaces from the left margin. Optional indentation is three to eight spaces, but five is preferred.

3. The subject line (if used) is typically centered on the page and occurs after the salutation.

4. Any optional letter part (or parts) may be used; if included, the part is blocked flush with the left margin.

5. Construction of individual letter parts should follow the guidelines for Modified Semi-Block letters listed in sections 4.1–4.14.

6. The Modified Semi-Block letter most often uses the mixed punctuation style. Open punctuation may be used, but it is not preferred.

2.5 HANGING-INDENT LETTER

The Hanging-Indent letter is a special-purpose format that is most popular in advertising letters. Its main feature is the unique paragraph alignment, designed to catch the reader's eye. Because of its special applications, the Hanging-Indent letter is limited in its optional letter parts and alternatives for placement of letter components chosen by the writer.

Special Features of the Hanging-Indent Letter

1. The date line, the complimentary closing, and the signature block are aligned with one another, with the longest of any of these letter parts flush with the right margin.

2. The reference line and the subject line are not used.

3. The first line of each paragraph and of the postscript (if used) are flush with the left margin. Subsequent lines in each paragraph and in the postscript are indented five spaces.

4. Other optional letter part (or parts) may be used; if included the part is blocked flush with the left margin. Construction of these latter parts is identical to those used in Block letters.

5. The Hanging-Indent letter uses either the open or the mixed punctuation style.

2.6 INDENTED LETTER

The Indented letter, though never used in business letter writing in the United States, may still be found in use among some European firms. It is included here as

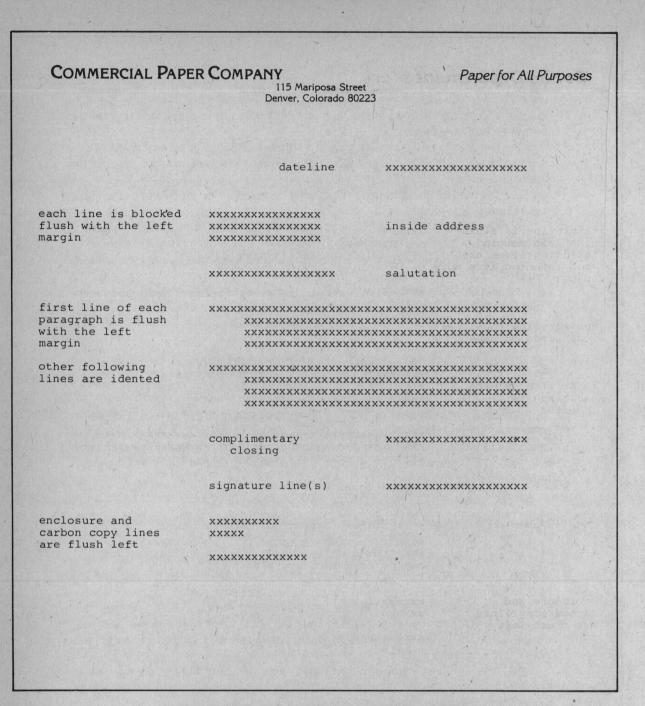

ILLUSTRATION 5. HANGING-INDENT LETTER

an example for correspondents who may encounter this letter format in communications with foreign firms.

Special Features of the Indented Letter

1. The date line ends flush with the right margin. The reference line, if used, is blocked directly above or below the date line, or it is centered on the page.

Dobbs Department Store
500 Cavalry Boulevard East
Canton, Ohio 44708

Service Since 1890

```
                        dateline           xxxxxxxxxxxxxxxxxx

first line is flush     xxxxxxxxxxxxxxxxx
with left margin            xxxxxxxxxxxxxxxx          inside address
following lines are             xxxxxxxxxxxxxxx
each indented five more
spaces

                        xxxxxxxxxxxxx              salutation

subject line (optional)         xxxxxxxxxxxxxxxxxxxxxxxx
   centered on page

                            xxxxxxxxxxxxxxxxxxxxxxxxxxxxxxxxxxxxxx
                        xxxxxxxxxxxxxxxxxxxxxxxxxxxxxxxxxxxxxxxxxx
first line of each      xxxxxxxxxxxxxxxxxxxxxxxxxxxxxxxxxxxxxxxxxx
paragraph is            xxxxxxxxxxxxxxxxxxxxxxxxxxxxxxxxxxxxxxxxxx
indented
                            xxxxxxxxxxxxxxxxxxxxxxxxxxxxxxxxxxxxxx
                        xxxxxxxxxxxxxxxxxxxxxxxxxxxxxxxxxxxxxxxxxx
                        xxxxxxxxxxxxxxxxxxxxxxxxxxxxxxxxxxxxxxxxxx
                        xxxxxxxxxxxxxxxxxxxxxxxxxxxxxxxxxxxxxxxxxx

                        complimentary          xxxxxxxxxxxxxxxxxx
                            closing

                        signature line(s) each    xxxxxxxxxxxxxx
                        indented five spaces         xxxxxxxxx
                        beyond complimentary closing

enclosure and           xxxxxxxxxxxx
carbon copy lines       xxxxx
are flush left
                        xxxxxxxxxxxxxx
```

ILLUSTRATION 6. INDENTED LETTER

2. The first line of the inside address is flush with the left margin. Subsequent lines are each indented five spaces more than the preceding line.

3. The subject line (if used) is centered on the page and is placed after the salutation.

4. The first line of each paragraph and the postscript (if used) are indented five spaces from the left margin. All other lines are flush with the left margin.

5. The signature block is indented five spaces beyond the complimentary closing, which begins at page center.

6. Other optional letter part or parts may be used; if included, the part is blocked flush with the left margin.

7. The Indented letter uses only the closed punctuation style.

```
              Keller Advertising Agency
                   160 East Grand Avenue
                   Chicago, Illinois 60603


                      dateline          xxxxxxxxxxxx


              xxxxxxxxxxxx
              xxxxxxxxxxxx          inside address
              xxxxxxxxxxxx


              xxxxxxxxxxxx          salutation


              xxxxxxxxxxxxxxxxxxxxxxxxxxxxxxxxxxxxxxx

paragraphs    xxxxxxxxxxxxxxxxxxxxxxxxxxxxxxxxxxxxxxx
are double
spaced throughout
              xxxxxxxxxxxxxxxxxxxxxxxxxxxxxxxxxxxxxxx

              xxxxxxxxxxxxxxxxxxxxxxxxxxxxxxxxxxxxxxx

              xxxxxxxxxxxxxxxxxxxxxxxxxxxxxxxxxxxxxxx


                    complimentary      xxxxxxxxxxxx
                      closing


                    signature          xxxxxxxxxxxx
                    line(s)
```

ILLUSTRATION 7. HALF-SHEET LETTER (BLOCK FORMAT SHOWN)

2.7 HALF-SHEET LETTER

The Half-Sheet letter is used for only extremely short notes; the message contained in this sort of letter should be no longer than two very short paragraphs. There is no specific styling used in a Half-Sheet letter, but the Full Block, Block, or Modified Semi-Block formats are all appropriate. Since the contents of this letter are quite limited by its brief size, optional letter parts used in the Half-Sheet letter should be restricted to those listed below.

Special Features of the Half-Sheet Letter

1. All Half-Sheet letters must include: the date line, the inside address, the salutation, the message, the complimentary closing, and the signature. Optional parts that may be used are: the reference line, the special mailing or on-arrival notation, the attention line, identification initials, the enclosure line, and the carbon copy distribution notation. If many or all of these optional parts must be used, it may be preferable to use a full-page version of a selected letter style.

2. Construction and placement of individual letter parts must follow the rules for the letter style that has been chosen for the Half-Sheet letter.

3. The Half-Sheet letter uses either the open or mixed punctuation style.

2.8 PUNCTUATION STYLES

Punctuation styles in modern business correspondence have changed over the years in ways similar to changes in letter format. Companies that have specific letter styles as a matter of general policy also require certain punctuation styles used in their letters. Just as the simpler, more efficient letter style has grown in popularity, the more modern punctuation styles gaining acceptance are also simple and streamlined. These newer punctuation patterns have replaced the more complex closed punctuation style in all letter forms except the rare and conservative Indented letter.

For each letter style, there are only one or two punctuation patterns appropriate for use with that style of letter. In order to quickly determine the preferred and optional punctuation patterns for the letter format you are using, see the following table:

LETTER STYLE	PUNCTUATION PATTERN		
	Closed	Mixed	Open
Simplified	No	No	Yes
Full Block	No	Either form optional	
Block	No	Either form optional	
Modified Semi-Block	No	Preferred	Optional
Hanging-Indent	No	Either form optional	
Indented	Yes	No	No

Whichever punctuation pattern is used should be followed consistently throughout the letter for accurate and fast reproduction of business correspondence.

Open Punctuation

Open punctuation is the simplest punctuation style used in modern business letters. Use of this punctuation pattern will simplify your typing chores; the Simplified letter uses this type of punctuation in order to produce business correspondence with a minimum number of keystrokes. These are the basic rules of the open punctuation style:

1. The end of the date line is unpunctuated. The comma between day and year is included.
2. The ends of lines of the inside address are unpunctuated, unless the line ends in an abbreviation that is terminated by a period. In this case, the period is included.
3. The salutation and the complimentary closing (if used) are unpunctuated.
4. The ends of the signature block lines are unpunctuated.
5. Optional letter parts (if used) contain no punctuation.

Mixed Punctuation

Mixed punctuation is a popular and preferred punctuation style suitable for most letter formats. A modification of the open punctuation pattern, it offers less ease in typing, but a more formal and conservative appearance. These are the basic rules of the mixed punctuation style:

1. The end of the date line is unpunctuated. The comma between day and year is included.
2. The ends of lines of the inside address are unpunctuated, unless the line ends in an abbreviation that is terminated by a period. In this case, the period is included.
3. The salutation is punctuated with a colon.
4. The complimentary closing is punctuated with a comma.
5. The ends of the signature block lines are unpunctuated.
6. Optional letter parts (if used) contain recommended punctuation, but are not terminated by punctuation marks.

Closed Punctuation

Closed punctuation is used exclusively in the Indented letter. Careful attention is required in order to correctly use the closed punctuation style consistently throughout a business letter. These are the basic rules of the closed punctuation style:

1. The end of the date line is punctuated with a period.
2. The ends of lines of the inside address are punctuated with commas, except the last line, which is terminated with a period.
3. The salutation is punctuated with a colon.

4. The complimentary closing is punctuated with a comma.

5. The ends of the signature block lines are punctuated with commas, except the last line, which is terminated with a period.

6. Optional letter parts (if used) are terminated with periods. If notations are used which cover more than one line, the first line or lines are terminated with commas, and the last line is terminated with a period.

This is how the three different punctuation styles would affect the date, inside address, salutation, complimentary closing, and signature block of a letter:

| | PUNCTUATION STYLE | |
Open	Mixed	Closed
May 31, 1957	May 31, 1957	May 31, 1957.
Mr. Donald Smith 67 Dean Street Orange, Iowa 11201	Mr. Donald Smith 67 Dean Street Orange, Iowa 11201	Mr. Donald Smith, 67 Dean Street, Orange, Iowa 11201.
Dear Mr. Smith	Dear Mr. Smith:	Dear Mr. Smith:
Sincerely yours	Sincerely yours,	Sincerely yours,
William James Personnel Manager	William James Personnel Manager	William James, Personnel Manager.

Unless company policy requires a certain letter format and punctuation style, selection of these characteristics for your own business correspondence is a matter of personal taste. But one thing that all modern business correspondence should have in common is an accepted letter style and punctuation pattern. If the rules for construction of business letters and their punctuation are carefully followed, readers will quickly and easily receive the messages those letters contain.

3

DESIGN AND PLACEMENT FOR MODERN LETTERS

The best business correspondence is attractively placed on the page, correctly laid out according to an accepted format, and neatly typed. The most difficult of these three qualities is the consistent symmetrical page placement for business letters of differing lengths. Your goal should be to create letters centered beneath the letterhead on each page, with equal margins at top and bottom. The overall appearance of business letters should be like attractively framed pictures: balanced on the page, surrounded by even margins.

3.1 PLACEMENT AND BALANCE FUNDAMENTALS

In order to produce attractive letters consistently, the most important thing to do is plan ahead. Before starting to type, a few simple steps will guarantee that the typed letter will be correctly and attractively placed on the page:

1. Estimate the approximate finished length of the letter. Use a rough draft or dictated notes to determine the number of words the message will contain.

2. List, in order, all quotations, charts, and special notations that will be included in the finished letter. Include their approximate lengths in estimations of letter length, and note any changes in margins or typeface that may be necessary.

3. Consult the Placement Guide in section 3.2 for recommended margin settings and spacing for the approximated letter length you are typing. Use a guide sheet or the calibrated platen on your typewriter to warn you that you are nearing the bottom margin.

4. Continuation sheet margins should be identical to those used on the first page of the letter.

3.2 PLACEMENT GUIDE

Based on the length of the messages they contain, letters can generally be divided into four categories:

1. Very Short Letters—50 words or less.
2. Short Letters—50 to 100 words.
3. Medium-length Letters—100 to 300 words.
4. Long Letters—300 words or more.

The length of a business letter determines the margin size, the preferred spacing between lines and paragraphs, and the number of pages the letter should cover. Using the estimated message length for your business letter, consult the table below to correctly place and balance the letter on a page.

LETTER LENGTH	PAGE NUMBER	MARGINS	SPACING
Very short—less than 50 words	Half-sheet	1″–1¼″	Double-spaced throughout
Short—50 to 100 words	One	Approx. 2″	Double-spaced throughout
Medium—100 to 300 words	One	1½″	Single-spaced within paragraphs, double-spaced between paragraphs
Long—300 words or more	Two or more	1″–1¼″	Single-spaced within paragraphs, double-spaced between paragraphs

These margin and spacing rules apply to continuation sheets as well as to first pages of letters. Once a margin and spacing style has been selected, the entire letter should be typed in that format. Top and bottom margins on each page should match the size of side margins for a balanced appearance in the finished product.

3.3 LETTERHEAD

Most business correspondence is sent on stationery that is imprinted with a corporate letterhead. The designs for letterhead vary from one firm to another: it may be laid out across the top of the page, centered on the page, biased to the top right or left on the page, or even split between the top and the bottom of the page.

Despite design differences in letterhead layout, all letterheads have certain elements in common. These are:

1. The complete name of the firm, corporation, institution, or group
2. The exact street address of the organization
3. The town or city, the state, and the ZIP code of the organization

In addition, letterheads may include:

1. Additional mailing information, such as room or building number and post office box number, if applicable
2. Telephone number or numbers, telex, or cable reference numbers
3. The name of a particular department, division, or group from which the correspondence originates, in the case of a large and diversified organization

Many organizations may also choose to include a corporate logo as part of its letterhead. In the search for a unique and distinctive stationery design, the logo is often placed at the bottom of the page on modern corporate letterhead.

Executive letterhead adds the name of an office (such as "Office of the President") or the full name of the officer and his or her business title (such as "Janet Smith, President") to the normal components of the letterhead. The name and office title are always placed directly below the top section of the letterhead, either at the left margin, or centered on the page. If the name and title are lengthy, they may be divided into two separate lines, blocked one above another. Frequently this sort of letterhead occurs on the Executive or Monarch size of stationery. These sizes of stationery are often of a higher-grade paper than the normal corporate stationery, and the letterhead on these special papers is engraved rather than printed.

3.4 CONTINUING SHEETS

Letters longer than three hundred words will occupy more than one page of final typed text. The pages following the first page of any letter are called *continuing sheets.* When stationery with a letterhead is used in correspondence, blank paper of the same weight, finish, and size is also supplied for use in lengthy letters. Only the first page of any business letter is typed on letterhead.

Continuing sheets of business letters should exhibit the same attention to good layout as first pages. To make continuing sheets an attractive and integrated part of your business correspondence, these rules should be followed:

1. Paper size, weight, and finish should be identical to that used on the first page of the letter.
2. Margins and spacing should match that used on the first page.
3. Letter format should be indentical to that used on the first page.
4. Continuing sheets should be correctly headed: six blank lines should be left above an accepted continuing sheet heading format. For those formats, see below.
5. Continuing sheets must contain at least three lines of message. The first and last word on each page should not be divided.

Continuing Sheet Heading Format: Simplified and Full Block Letter Styles

In the Simplified and Full Block letter styles, the continuing sheet heading is blocked flush left six lines from the top of the page. The heading will vary in form only if a reference number is used on the first page of the letter. If a reference line is included on the first page of a Full Block letter, it should be included on all continuing sheets.

No reference line
Mr. Meade	*reader's name / company's name*
Page 2	*page number*
August 10, 19 ___	*date*

With reference line
Mr. Meade	*reader's name / company's name*
August 10, 19 ___	*date*
Ref. 35-218	*reference line as it appears on page 1*
Page 2	*page number*

This heading is single-spaced internally, and the first message line on the continuing sheet should begin four lines below the final line of the continuing sheet heading.

Continuing Sheet Heading Format: All Other Letter Styles

In the Block, Modified Semi-Block, Hanging-Indent, and Indented letter styles, the continuing sheet heading is laid out on a single line six lines from the top of the page. If a reference line is included on the first page, it should be included on all continuing sheets, one space above or below the date. Placement of the reference line should duplicate its placement on the first page.

No reference line
Mr. Meade	- 2 -	August 10, 19 ___

With reference line below
Mr. Meade	- 2 -	August 10, 19 ___
		Ref. 35-218

With reference line above
Mr. Meade	- 2 -	Ref. 35-218
		August 10, 19 ___

If the reference line is centered on the first page, on continuing sheets it should be blocked flush with the right margin below the date.

In this heading format, the reader's or the company's name is flush with the left margin, the page number is centered on the page and surrounded by spaced hyphens, and the date (and the reference line, if used) is flush with the right margin. The first message line should begin four lines below the final line of the continuing sheet heading.

3.5 HALF-SHEET LETTER BALANCE AND PLACEMENT

The Half-Sheet letter, used only for extremely brief notes, is typed on paper of Baronial size, 5½″ x 8½″. Since the majority of corporate letterhead is Standard- or Executive-size, Half-Sheet letters are often typed on stationery without letterhead. When non-letterhead stationery is used, the address/date block should begin six lines from the top of the page. If letterhead is used, the date line should be placed as listed in section 4.1.

Because of the small size of the stationery used in the Half-Sheet letter, certain rules of placement and margin-sizing must be followed in order to produce a balanced and attractive letter. These rules are:

1. Margins must be no less than 1″ at each side, and no more than 1¼″.
2. Three lines should separate the date line from the inside address. Two blank lines should separate the inside address from the salutation.
3. The message contained in the letter must be double-spaced throughout.

If it becomes apparent that a letter typed on Baronial stationery is too long for the paper's small size, then it is advisable to retype the letter using Standard-size stationery and a spacing and margin selection appropriate to its length.

Good correspondence should never look crowded or cramped by the size of the stationery. With practice following the rules listed in this chapter, letter balance and placement will become fast, easy, and a natural part of your business skills.

4

PARTS OF THE BUSINESS LETTER

Business letters are composed of a number of individual working parts. While all letters have certain parts in common, a number of other letter components are used depending on the letter format (as with Simplified or Full Block) or the character of the letter (personal or confidential correspondence, special enclosures, and so on). These are the parts of modern business letters, in order of appearance in modern correspondence:

PARTS OF THE BUSINESS LETTER

Always Used	Optional
1. Date line	
2.	Reference line
3.	Special mailing notations and on-arrival notations
4. Inside address	
5.	Attention line
6.	Salutation
7.	Subject line
8. Message	
9.	Complimentary closing
10. Signature block	
11.	Identification initials
12.	Enclosure lines
13.	Carbon copy notation
14.	Postscript

When writing business letters, the rules for construction, content, and placement of these letter parts should be carefully followed. Be sure to note that some of these letter components vary in form and placement for differing letter formats.

4.1 DATE LINE

The date line is the first letter part of all business correspondence. The date line is typed two to six lines beneath the bottom of the letterhead; the most common spacing is three lines below the letterhead. In short, single-page letters, the larger spacing is preferable. Placement on the page may be flush left, flush right, centered,

23

or five spaces right of page center. This placement is determined by the letter format chosen for the correspondence.

When stationery without letterhead is used for business correspondence, the date line is supplemented by the street address, city, state, and ZIP code from where the letter originates. These lines are blocked directly above the date line as shown:

Street address	56 Deerfield Lane
City, state, ZIP code	Betheny, CT 06525
Date line	August 11, 19 __

When using this form, the first line begins six to ten lines from the top of the page, depending upon the letter's length. The three lines are single-spaced internally. Other rules for the construction of the address and the date lines are:

1. In the address, the words *street* and *avenue* are not abbreviated. Names of cities or towns are spelled out in full. States may be abbreviated using the U.S. Postal Service two-letter abbreviations listed in Chapter 8. Postal or ZIP codes must be used.

2. Street numbers are spelled out up to ten; street numbers are written in numerals above ten. Do not add *th, rd,* or *st* to numbers of streets or days of the month. Months should be spelled out in full.

3. House numbers are written in numerals, except the number *one*, which is always spelled out.

4. A comma is always used between the city and the state, and between the day of the month and the year, no matter what punctuation pattern is used in the letter.

The four placements for date lines are listed and illustrated below. Be sure to use the placement recommended for the letter format you have chosen for your correspondence.

1. Date line blocked flush with left margin—used with the Simplified and Full Block letter styles.

August 11, 19 __

2. Date line blocked flush with right margin—used with the Block, Modified Semi-Block, Hanging-Indent, and Indented letter styles. The final digit of the date is aligned exactly with the right margin.

August 11, 19 __

3. Date line centered on the page—optional for use with the Block and Modified Semi-Block letter styles.

August 11, 19 __

4. Date line five spaces right of page center—optional for use with the Block and Modified Semi-Block letter styles.

August 11, 19 __

(See section 3.4 for date line placement on continuing sheets.)

4.2 REFERENCE LINE

The reference line, an optional part of the business letter, is placed on the page immediately above or below the date line. When correspondence is devoted to a certain file, policy, order or invoice, or intended for filing purposes, the reference line serves as a useful tool for both the reader and the writer of the correspondence.

Three placements are acceptable for reference lines in letters. If the date line is blocked flush left, the reference line is also blocked flush left, one space above or below the date line. If the date line is centered on the page, five spaces right of page center, or flush right on the page, the reference line may either be blocked one space directly above or below the date, or centered on the page four lines below the date.

Construction of reference lines may vary greatly. It is acceptable to simply list a file, order, or invoice number as a reference line:

August 11, 19 __
B-25295

Or you can precede the number with a phrase such as: Your file number, Your reference; or Reference (spelled out or abbreviated). These phrases or words should begin with a capital letter and be punctuated with a colon. See the examples listed below:

1. Reference line blocked flush left—used with the Full Block letter style; may appear above or below the date line.

August 11, 19 __   *Reference line below date*
Ref. B-25295

Ref. B-25295   *Reference line above date*
August 11, 19 __

2. Reference line blocked above or below date at page center, five spaces right of page center, or flush right—used with the Block, Modified Semi-Block, Hanging-Indent, and Indented letter styles.

Blocked below, *at page center*	August 11, 19 __ B-25295
Blocked above, *at page center*	B-25295 August 11, 19 __
Blocked below, five spaces *right of page center*	August 11, 19 __ Your reference: B-25295

Blocked above, five spaces right of page center	Your reference: B-25295 August 11, 19 —

Blocked below,
flush right
    August 11, 19 —
    B-25295

Blocked above,
flush right
    B-25295
    August 11, 19 —

3. Reference line centered on the page, four lines below the date line—optionally used with the Block, Modified Semi-Block, Hanging-Indent, and Indented letter styles. Centering is preferred when the reference line is lengthy and the date line is blocked flush right.

                                                 August 11, 19 —

                     In reply, refer to file No. 25295

If the reference line is centered on the first page of a letter, on continuing sheets the reference line should be blocked flush right below the date and shortened to a simple number or code. (For continuing-sheet headings with reference lines, see section 3.4.)

4.3 SPECIAL MAILING AND ON-ARRIVAL NOTATIONS

Placed four lines beneath the date line or the reference line, special mailing and on-arrival notations may be used to specify a delivery method and intended readers for a business letter. Because of their purpose, these lines, if used in a letter, are also included on the envelope. (See section 8.2 for use and placement of these lines on envelopes.)

Special mailing notations are used only if a letter is to be delivered by other than regular mail. An all-capitalized notation, such as CERTIFIED or SPECIAL DELIVERY, is aligned flush left on the page four lines beneath the last preceding line.

On-arrival notations are used to indicate which reader or readers are authorized to view the material enclosed. PERSONAL is used when the letter should only be read by its addressee. CONFIDENTIAL is used when the letter may be read by its addressee and other persons authorized to view material the letter contains. These notations, all-capitalized and aligned flush left, appear four lines below the preceding line if no special mailing notation is present. In the case where both special mailing *and* on-arrival notations are included, the mailing notation appears four lines below the last preceding line on the page, and the on-arrival notation is blocked one line directly below.

August 11, 19 —   *Date line*

SPECIAL DELIVERY   *Mailing notation*
PERSONAL   *On-arrival notation*

Mr. Donald Jay
67 Deerfield Lane   *Inside address*
Columbus, Ohio 43215

4.4 INSIDE ADDRESS

Used in all business letters, the inside address gives the name, title, and exact address of the person to whom the letter is addressed. If a specific person is not the addressee, either the name of a firm or a department within that firm may be used. The inside address is placed two to six lines below the last preceding line on the page; if only a date line appears above the inside address, three to eight lines is the optional spacing between the date line and the inside address. In most cases, three lines is the preferred spacing; however, it is the mandatory spacing in the Simplified letter.

The inside address must occupy three to five lines, single-spaced. In all letter formats except the Indented letter, the inside address is blocked flush with the left margin. (See section 2.6 for construction of the inside address in Indented letters.)

Inside addresses of letters directed to specific individuals include:

First line—Addressee's courtesy title and full name
Second line—Addressee's business title*
Third line—Full name of business or organization†
Fourth line—Number, street, and room of business
Fifth line— City, state, and ZIP code *or*
           City, state, country, and postal code

Whenever a business letter is addressed to an individual or individuals, a courtesy title such as Mr., Ms., Miss, Mrs., Dr., or special title should be typed before the addressee's full name, even if a business title appears on the following line. (See Chapter 5 for general styles for multiple addressees and cases when special titles are used with individuals' names in inside addresses.)

The addressee's name and business title, in spelling and in construction, should match as closely as possible the signature block or the executive letterhead of previous correspondence from the individual. If the business title is long enough to overrun the center of the page when placed on a single line of an inside address, it should be divided onto two lines, with the second line indented two spaces. Business titles must never be abbreviated in the inside address.

EXAMPLES OF INSIDE ADDRESSES FOR INDIVIDUALS

Mr. Anthony Small
64 Gerdes Avenue
Verona, New Jersey 07044   *For a private individual*

---

* If the addressee has no specific business title, this line may be omitted.
†If the addressee is not affiliated with a business or organization, this line may be omitted.

Ms. Geraldine Temple
Director of Marketing
Federated Motor Company
30 Industrial Way   *For a businessperson*
Dallas, Texas 72511   *affiliated with a firm*

Mr. Donald Barclay
United Producers
762 Calvary Street   *For a businessperson with*
Madison, WI 53711   *no company title*

Ms. Anna Skye, Director
Social Services Bureau
865 Willow Street   *Optional form used with*
Brooklyn, NY 11201   *short business titles*

Mr. Davis Land
President, Alpha Realty
334 Merton Street   *Optional form used with short*
Hollywood, California 90046   *business name and title*

A business title following the addressee's name or preceding the company or organization name, but on the same line, is recommended if the title is not lengthy. This form is suitable for use with all letter formats.

Inside addresses of letters directed to firms or departments of firms include:

First line—Full name of business or organization
Second line—Name of department, if necessary
Third line—Number, street, and room of business
Fourth line— City, state, and ZIP code *or*
　　　　　　　 City, state, country, and postal code

The name of the organization, in spelling and construction, should be exactly as it appears in the organization's letterhead, or as it appears in business directories. If a specific person is being addressed in a firm or an organization, but that individual's name is unknown or unnecessary in the correspondence, his or her job title (such as ''Director of Personnel'') should appear on the first line of the inside address, the business' or organization's name should appear on the second line, and the address of the organization should appear on the third and fourth lines.

EXAMPLES OF INSIDE ADDRESSES FOR FIRMS AND ORGANIZATIONS

Association of Business Services
455 Appalachian Way   *For an organization or*
Louisville, KY 40213   *business*

Innovative Play Products
Customer Service Department
355 Weybosset, Suite 1900   *For a department of an*
Providence, Rhode Island 02903   *organization or business*

Director of Personnel
Legrath Associates
56 Globe Avenue   *For an unknown person*
South Bend, Indiana 46613   *with a specific title*

Whether business correspondence is addressed to an individual or a firm, construction of addresses should follow these rules:

1. The words *street* or *avenue* are not abbreviated. Names of cities and towns are spelled out in full. States may be abbreviated using the U.S. Postal Service two-letter abbreviations listed in Chapter 9. Postal or ZIP codes must be used.
2. Street numbers are spelled out up to ten; street numbers above ten are written in numerals. Do not add *th, rd,* or *st* to street numbers when numerals are used.
3. House numbers are written in numerals, except the number *one,* which is spelled out.
4. A comma is used between the city and the state, and between the street address and the room / floor number, if used. A comma is also used to separate the addressee's name and the business title or the business title and the business' or organization's name, if both are placed on the same inside address line. (See the optional formats illustrated above.)
5. If no street address is available for an individual or a business, the city and the state should be typed on separate lines to expand the inside address to three typed lines.

4.5 ATTENTION LINE

If you need to direct business correspondence addressed to a business or an organization to a specific individual, the attention line should be used. Placed flush left, the attention line is located two lines beneath the inside address, and two lines above the salutation or, in the case of the Simplified letter, two lines above the subject line.

Acceptable formats for the attention line are:

Attention Mr. Jules Scott   *Suitable for all letter and*
                                 punctuation styles

Attention: Ms. Anna Serle   *Optional for use with mixed*
                                 punctuation

Attention lines are neither completely capitalized nor underlined. Main elements present in attention lines are capitalized. A colon may be used if the mixed punctuation style is being followed throughout the letter.

4.6 SALUTATION

Used with all letter styles except the Simplified letter, the salutation or greeting is always placed flush left two to four lines below the last preceding letter part (inside address or attention line). The first and last words and all nouns, names, and courtesy titles used in the salutation are capitalized. If open punctuation is used in the letter, the salutation is unpunctuated. Other punctuation styles terminate the salutation with a colon.

Salutations Directed to Specific Individuals

In business correspondence directed to individuals, certain forms of salutation have become customary. The use of a specific form of greeting is determined by the familiarity existing between the writer and the reader:

1. Unknown individual—This salutation is used when the reader is a specific individual whose name is not known to the writer.

2. Unfamiliar reader—This salutation is used when the name of the reader is known, but little or no prior correspondence has passed between the writer and the reader.

3. Personal—This salutation is used when a great deal of correspondence has passed between the writer and the reader, or personal contact has been established.

SALUTATIONS DIRECTED TO INDIVIDUALS

READER FAMILIARITY	FEMALE READER	MALE READER
Unknown individual	Dear Madam:	Dear Sir:
Unfamiliar reader	Dear Ms./Miss/Mrs. Smith: (use reader's courtesy title and last name)	Dear Mr. Smith:
Personal	Dear Anna: (use reader's first name)	Dear Ralph:

(See Chapter 5 for salutations for multiple addressees and individual readers who require special greetings.) If in doubt about how to address an individual in the salutation of a business letter, it is best to be less familiar rather than too personal.

Salutations Directed to Firms or Organizations

In business correspondence directed to a firm or organization, the modern salutation has been frequently restyled. The interest in equal rights and opportunities for both sexes has played a large part in the modifications made to the traditional salutation. You should choose a salutation which best fits your personal or corporate correspondence:

SALUTATIONS DIRECTED TO FIRMS OR ORGANIZATIONS

TRADITIONAL	MODERN	UNCONVENTIONAL
*Gentlemen:	*Ladies and Gentlemen:	*Gentlepersons:
Dear Sirs:	Dear Sir or Madam:	Dear People:
*Ladies: Mesdames:		Dear Sir, Madam, or Ms.:

*recommended styling

4.7 SUBJECT LINE

The subject line is a valuable feature of a business letter. It is always used in Simplified-style letters, and it is optionally used in all other letter styles. Blocked flush left two lines below the salutation (three lines below the inside address or the attention line in Simplified letters), the subject line serves to quickly and briefly indicate the matter addressed by the correspondence. In modern business letters, the subject line will help to streamline correspondence with its summarized message. Filing of letters with subject lines is also much faster and easier.

Subject lines, because of their purpose, should be short—no more than a single line. In all cases, the subject line should either be completely capitalized or underlined with the main words capitalized.

The subject line format for all letter styles is governed by the punctuation pattern chosen for the letter. When open punctuation is used with any of these letter formats, the word *SUBJECT* is deleted, and the topic statement stands alone and is unpunctuated:

August 11, 19 __

Able Shoe Company
456 Dillon Drive
New York, N.Y. 10017   *Full Block Style*

Gentlemen

SHOE REPLACEMENT WARRANTY

This style of subject line (and punctuation format) is always used in Simplified letters.

If mixed or closed punctuation is chosen for your letter style, then the subject line is introduced with the word *SUBJECT* terminated with a colon.

August 11, 19 __

Able Shoe Company
456 Dillon Drive
New York, N.Y. 10017

Gentlemen:

SUBJECT: SHOE REPLACEMENT WARRANTY

The unheaded style of subject line is also acceptable, but not preferred, when using these punctuation styles in correspondence.

4.8 MESSAGE

The message or body of a business letter is organized according to letter style, length, and content. Since the text of a letter is the focus of business correspondence, special attention should be paid to clear, careful construction and thoughtful writing style, regardless of the letter's format, length, or purpose.

The message of a letter should begin two lines below the salutation or two lines below the subject line (if used) in all letter styles except the Simplified letter; in the Simplified letter, the message begins three lines beneath the subject line. Margins for business letters should be sized according to letter length and the rules listed in Chapter 3.

Paragraphs are blocked flush left in the Simplified, Full Block, and Block letters. In Indented and Modified Semi-Block letters, the first typed line of each paragraph is indented five spaces right of the left margin, and all following lines are blocked flush left. In Hanging-Indent letters, the first typed line of each paragraph is flush left, and all following lines are indented about five spaces to the right.

Medium-length and long letters are single-spaced within paragraphs and double-spaced between paragraphs. Short letters may be double-spaced throughout. Quotations longer than fifty words should be set off from the text by double-spacing at the top and bottom and indenting all lines within the quotation five spaces from the right and the left margins. Long quotations should be single-spaced internally.

Lists (enumerations) should also be indented and blocked five spaces from the right and left margins. Items should be single-spaced internally if they cover more than one line apiece, and double-spaced between items. Charts or tables, if included in the body of a letter, should be centered on the page.

Long letters that require one or more continuing sheets should be consistent in format, spacing, and margins from one page to the next. A continuing sheet must contain at least three lines of text. The complimentary closing and the signature block should never stand alone on the last page of a business letter. (See section 3.4 for details of continuing-sheet heading formats.)

4.9 COMPLIMENTARY CLOSING

Used in all letters, except those constructed in the Simplified format, the complimentary closing is placed two lines beneath the end of the message. In Full Block-style letters, the complimentary closing is blocked flush left with all other letter parts. In the other letter format styles, the complimentary closing is placed directly beneath the date line—either flush with the right margin, centered on the page, or five spaces right of page center. The complimentary closing should never overrun the right margin.

The first word of every complimentary closing is capitalized. When closed or mixed punctuation is used, the closing is terminated by a comma. In open punctuation, the comma is omitted in the complimentary closing.

Like the salutation, the style of the complimentary closing is determined by the familiarity existing between the writer and the reader:

1. Unknown individual—These closings are polite and neutral in tone, and are used in general correspondence.

2. Unfamiliar reader—These closings are less formal and more personal, and are used in general correspondence and letters when the writer and the reader are known to each other.

3. Personal—These closings are informal, and are used when the reader and the writer are on a first-name basis.

Of course, there are individuals who merit special salutations and complimentary closings because of their title or office. (See Chapter 5 for a complete listing of these individuals and appropriate salutations and complimentary closings.)

COMPLIMENTARY CLOSINGS FOR MOST BUSINESS CORRESPONDENCE

READER FAMILIARITY	FORMAL	PERSONAL
Unknown individual	Yours truly, Yours very truly, Very truly yours,	Sincerely, Sincerely yours, Very sincerely yours, Most sincerely, Most sincerely yours,
Unfamiliar reader	Sincerely, Sincerely yours, Very sincerely yours, Most sincerely, Most sincerely yours,	Cordially, Cordially yours, Most cordially, Yours cordially,
Personal	Cordially, Cordially yours, Most cordially, Yours cordially,	Yours, Your friend, As ever, Best regards, Regards,

For readers who you feel deserve more recognition or formality, standard forms of closing are:

Respectfully,
Respectfully yours,
Very respectfully,
Most respectfully,

These examples illustrate the three most common placements for complimentary closings used in business letters:

Yours truly,   *Blocked at left margin*

James D. Franklin

Executive Signature
Title

Five spaces right of center   Sincerely yours,

James D. Franklin

Executive Signature
Title

Flush with right margin   Most sincerely yours,

Harry Gellins

Signature
Title

Certain traditional forms of complimentary closing are outdated and unacceptable. These include:

Obediently yours,
Humbly yours,
Expecting your early reply, I am,
I remain, your humble servant,
Thanking you in advance, I remain,

If a letter is typed from dictation, it is important for the typist to use the complimentary closing exactly as it was dictated because the writer may intend the closing to set a certain tone of formality or informality for the correspondence. If no specific closing is indicated, it is the responsibility of the typist to select a closing which fits in well with the general tone of the letter and the relationship between the writer and the intended reader of the correspondence.

4.10 SIGNATURE BLOCK

The signature block is used in all business letter formats. Construction and page placement is dependent upon the format used for the specific letter you are writing or typing. In general, all signature blocks include:

1. At least four lines open for the writer's signature.
2. The writer's name.
3. The writer's business title, if necessary.

Simplified Letter Signature Block

In letters typed in the Simplified letter format, the signature block is a single line typed flush left and completely capitalized. This line is placed five lines beneath the final line of the message:

xxxxxxxxxxxxxxxxxxx END OF MESSAGE xxxxxxxxxxxxxxx.

Marc Rogers

MARC ROGERS

If the writer's business title is not included in the printed letterhead, then his or her title may be included on the same line as the writer's name, set off with a spaced hyphen, and completely capitalized:

xxxxxxxxxxxxxxxxx END OF MESSAGE xxxxxxxxxxxxx.

Marc Rogers

MARC ROGERS – CHIEF ELECTRICIAN

If the writer's business title is long or complex, a second line may be added to complete the business title:

xxxxxxxxxxxxxxxxxx END OF MESSAGE xxxxxxxxxxxxxxx.

Marc Rogers

MARC ROGERS – CHIEF ELECTRICIAN
OPERATIONS MANAGEMENT CENTER

The typed name of the writer should include any academic or professional degrees if they are not included on the printed letterhead but are necessary in the correspondence. Signatures should never include courtesy, academic, or professional titles.

Full Block Letter Signature Block

In letters typed in the Full Block format, the signature block is flush left four lines beneath the complimentary closing. Only the first letter of each major element in the writer's name, title, and department is capitalized:

xxxxxxxxxxxxxxxxxxxxxx END OF MESSAGE xxxxxxxxxxxxxxx.

Yours truly,

Ann Paterno

Ann Paterno

If the company and the department name are included in the letterhead, then the business title of the writer should be placed on a second line immediately below the writer's name. If space permits, you may include the title on the same line as the writer's name, separated by a comma:

xxxxxxxxxxxxxxxxxxxx END OF MESSAGE xxxxxxxxxxxxxxx.

Yours truly,

Ann Paterno

Ann Paterno
Director

xxxxxxxxxxxxxxxxxxxx END OF MESSAGE xxxxxxxxxxxxxxxx.

Yours truly,

Ann Paterno

Ann Paterno, Director

When both the title and the department name are needed for identification, then the writer's name and title should be placed on the first line, followed by the department name:

xxxxxxxxxxxxxxxxxxxxx END OF MESSAGE xxxxxxxxxxxxxxxx.

Yours truly,

Ann Paterno

Ann Paterno, Director
Consumer Testing Division

The typed name of the writer should include any academic or professional degrees if they are necessary but are not included on the printed letterhead. Signatures should never include courtesy, academic, or professional titles.

Block, Modified Semi-Block, and Hanging-Indent Signature Block

Letters in the Block, Modified Semi-Block, and Hanging-Indent formats all have similar signature block construction and placement. The signature block begins four lines below the complimentary closing, with the first letter of each line of the signature block aligned with the first letter of the complimentary closing. If any line of the signature block will overrun the right margin (this is possible when the date and the complimentary closing are blocked flush right), then you may either center the signature block beneath the complimentary closing or place the signature block so that the longest line of the signature block ends flush with the right margin, and all other lines used in the block begin directly above or below the first letter of the longest line:

xxxxxxxxxxxxxxxxxxxx END OF MESSAGE xxxxxxxxxxxxxx.

Very sincerely yours,

James D. Franklin

James D. Franklin, Director
Jones-Franklin Communications Corp.

xxxxxxxxxxxxxxxxxx END OF MESSAGE xxxxxxxxxxxxxxx.

Very sincerely yours,

James D. Franklin

James D. Franklin, Director
Jones-Franklin Communications Corp.

Rules for inclusion of titles and capitalization within the signature blocks of these letter styles are indentical to those used in Full Block letters.

Signature Blocks: Special Cases

In signature blocks of all letter styles, certain general rules help to specify what should be included in the signature block and how writers should sign letters in special cases:

1. In cases where non-letterhead stationery is used in a general corporate letter to an individual, the writer's signature should be preceded by a corporate name, completely capitalized, two lines beneath the complimentary closing. The typed lines of the signature block then begin four lines beneath the corporate name:

Full Block format

Very truly yours,

DELTA CHEMICAL CORPORATION

Harry Gellins

Harry Gellins
President

Other formats

Very truly yours,

DELTA CHEMICAL CORPORATION

Harry Gellins

Harry Gellins
President

2. Women—married, unmarried, or widowed—should always sign their names without a courtesy title. The courtesy title may be included in the typed name on the line below. These are the options for women writers of business letters:

Yours truly,

Universal—no marital status indicated

Sally Freed
Director

Yours truly,

Universal—no marital status indicated

(Ms.) Sally Freed
Director

Yours truly,

Optionally used by an unmarried woman

(Miss) Sally Freed
Director

Yours truly,

Optionally used by a married woman

(Mrs.) Sally Freed

Yours truly,

Used by a married woman using her husband's full name

Mrs. Daniel Freed
Director

Note that the signature is always the same, even if the woman intends to use her husband's full name.

    3. Academic degrees and professional titles are included on the first line of the typed signature, but not in the written signature. The title or degree may be preceded by a comma:

Yours truly,

Sally Freed, Ph.D.
Director

These titles and degrees indicate to readers how you wish to be addressed by them in the salutation of their correspondence.

4. A typist who signs correspondence for someone else should indicate that fact by placing his or her (the typist's) initials to the bottom right of the signature, in his or her own handwriting:

Yours truly,

James T. Williams

James T. Williams   B.C.
Vice-President

5. When a letter is signed by a secretary or assistant in his or her own name, that person should compose the signature block with his or her own signature, name, and exact title:

Yours truly,

Jeremy Kopit

Jeremy Kopit
Assistant to Mr. Williams

6. Punctuation of signature blocks should be consistent with the punctuation used throughout the letter. (See section 2.8 for samples of signature block punctuation patterns.)

4.11 IDENTIFICATION INITIALS

When a letter is dictated and typed by different individuals, the typist is identified by initials placed two lines beneath the signature block. If the typist also signs the letter in his or her own name, the initials of the person who dictated the letter are typed first, in capitals, followed by a colon and the initials of the letter's typist in lower case. The identification initials are always blocked flush left:

Sandra T. Olson
Manager

anf

*Dictated letter typed by
a secretary or assistant*

Edna Delbert
Assistant to Ms. Olson

STO:ed

*Letter typed and
signed by an assistant or
secretary*

Note that it is preferred that the typist's initials are in lower case, even if the writer's initials are not included in the identification line.

4.12 ENCLOSURE LINES

If a business letter is to include a separate enclosure or enclosures, a notation of that fact is typed immediately below the identification initials (if present), or two lines beneath the signature block (if no identification initials are present). The enclosure line or lines are always blocked flush left. If more than a single enclosure line is necessary, the lines are single-spaced internally.

Popular formats for enclosure lines use either the words *Enclosure* or *Enclosures,* or their abbreviation *Enc., enc., Encl.,* or *encl.* Capitalization of the first letter is preferred only if the word is spelled out fully. If multiple enclosures are to be included, the count of those items is placed in parentheses after *Enclosures* or *encls.:*

Enclosure
   or   *For a single enclosure*
encl.

Enclosures (5)
   or   *For multiple enclosures*
encls. (5)

When it is necessary to include important multiple enclosures in a business letter, it is often a good idea to list them by name and number, and either attach a cover sheet with the identification number and the date of the letter to the enclosure, or type on the enclosure its identifying number and the date of its cover letter:

Enclosures: 1. List of Land Acquisitions, 19 ___
           2. Profitability Study, West Woods, 19 ___
           3. Financing Study, January 19 ___
Enclosure (1) to (addressee's name)   *Information on cover sheets*
        dated: (date on letter)   *for above enclosures*

4.13 CARBON COPY NOTATION

Carbon copies should be kept of all business correspondence. When a copy is made to be sent to another individual, it is customary to note that fact with a carbon copy notation. This notation is flush left, and begins two lines beneath the preceding letter part. If the carbon copy distribution notation covers more than a single line, all lines should be single-spaced internally.

The most common styles for carbon copy notations are:

cc   cc: Copy to   Copies to

The initials of the recipient(s) of the copies follow the notation:

cc: DLK   Copies to DXW
    EGT   *or*   BBA
    FCM   CYX

If you feel it would be useful for the addressee of the original letter, you may include the recipient's full name and address.

The blind carbon copy notation is used when the writer does not wish the addressee to know that copies are being distributed to other individuals. Instead of cc:, bcc: is used, and it is only placed on the copies of the letter, not the original. The format is the same. Placement of the blind copy notation may be at the top left corner on the first page of copies for internal use.

4.14 POSTSCRIPT

When a postscript is used, it is placed two to four lines below the last notation, and single-spaced throughout. Margins and paragraph alignment should match the paragraph construction used in the body of the letter. The writer should always initial the postscript. Modern letters frequently do not label postscripts with P.S.. Since the notation P.S. is unnecessary and space-consuming, it is recommended that you keep postscripts unlabeled in your correspondence.

5

SPECIAL ADDRESSES, SALUTATIONS, AND COMPLIMENTARY CLOSINGS

Most business letters are addressed and directed to a specific person or company. The standard procedure for constructing the inside address, the salutation, and the complimentary closing for this type of letter is listed in Chapter 4. When an addressee is an important person (or more than one person), a different form of salutation and complimentary closing, and possibly a different form of inside address, is needed. This chapter is a guide for using special forms of inside addresses, salutations, and complimentary closings.

The following sections cover the various forms of special addresses, salutations, and complimentary closings for the following addressees:

1. General styles for important persons, multiple addressees, and persons with special titles
2. Members of the clergy and religious orders
3. Diplomatic and public officials
4. School officials and faculty
5. Military personnel

Find the section which best describes your special addressee. Use the information provided to construct an effective and appropriate address, salutation, and complimentary closing. In general, the listings provided are for individuals who are unfamiliar to the writer. If you should have personal knowledge of the addressee, use a less formal form of address or written reference, if it is appropriate.

5.1 GENERAL STYLES

Forms of address and salutation for important individuals, multiple addressees, and persons with special titles vary according to organizational and personal taste. Below are suggested formats for these letter parts in special business correspondence.

Important Persons

Diplomats, high government officials, and important public figures all require an appropriate form of salutation and complimentary closing. If the individual is not among those listed in the charts in sections 5.2–5.5, then you should use an appropriate general form of address in correspondence with this person. The recommended formats for address, salutation, complimentary closing, and manner of oral or written reference follow:

ADDRESS: Courtesy title and name
Position or post
Mailing address and ZIP code

SALUTATION: Sir or Madam (Madame for foreign addressee)
Dear Mr. / Mrs. / Ms. / Miss (position or post)
Dear Mr. / Mrs. / Ms. / Miss (name)
Dear Mr. / Madam (position or post)

COMPLIMENTARY CLOSING: Respectfully or Respectfully yours (especially courteous)
Very sincerely yours
Very truly yours

ORAL OR WRITTEN REFERENCE: (position or post) (name)
Mr. / Madam (position or post)
Mr. / Mrs. / Ms. / Miss (name)

Multiple Addressees

Letters written to more than one specific individual present special problems for the construction of the inside address and salutation. Since the combination of persons a letter may be addressed to are infinite, a good general rule of construction for inside addresses and salutations is to list each person to whom the letter is addressed separately in the address and the salutation. Use each person's courtesy title and full name in the inside address; use the same courtesy title and the individual's last name in the salutation.

Below is a listing of common combinations of individuals to whom business letters may be directed. Use this listing as a guide for the construction of inside addresses and salutations in letters with multiple addressees. If you have any doubt about using a combination form (like Mesdames or Messrs.), revert to the general style of separate listings described above.

MARRIED COUPLE
ADDRESS: Mr. and Mrs. (surname)   *Preferred*
mailing address and ZIP code   *styling*

Mr. and Ms. (surname)   *More*
mailing address and ZIP code   *contemporary*

Mr. and Mrs. (man's name)   *More*
mailing address and ZIP code   *traditional*

(man's and woman's name) (surname)
mailing address and ZIP code   *Optional*

SALUTATION: Dear Mr. and Mrs. (surname)   *Preferred*

Dear Mr. and Ms. (surname)   *Contemporary*

Dear (first names)   *Personal*

TWO OR MORE MEN—SAME SURNAME

ADDRESS: Mr. (name)
Mr. (name)
mailing address and ZIP code

Messrs. (first names divided by commas) (surname)
mailing address and ZIP code

Messrs. (first name initials divided by commas) (surname)
mailing address and ZIP code

SALUTATION: Dear Messrs. (surname)

Gentlemen

TWO OR MORE MEN—DIFFERENT SURNAMES

ADDRESS: Mr. (name)
Mr. (name)
mailing address and ZIP code

Messrs. (surname 1) and (surname 2)
mailing address and ZIP code

Messrs. (full name) and (full name)
mailing address and ZIP code

SALUTATION: Dear Mr. (surname 1) and Mr. (surname 2)

Dear Messrs. (surname 1) and (surname 2)

Gentlemen:

TWO OR MORE WOMEN—INDETERMINATE OR UNIMPORTANT MARITAL STATUS

ADDRESS: Ms. (name)
Ms. (name)
mailing address and ZIP code

Ms. (first names divided by commas) (surname)
mailing address and ZIP code
(for women with the same surname)

SALUTATION: Dear Ms. (surname) and Ms. (surname)

Dear Ms. (first names divided by commas) (surname)
(for women with the same surname)

TWO OR MORE MARRIED WOMEN

ADDRESS: Mrs. (name)
Mrs. (name)
mailing address and ZIP code

Mesdames (full name) and (full name)
mailing address and ZIP code

Mesdames (first names divided by commas) (surname)
mailing address and ZIP code
                        (For women with the same surname)

SALUTATION: Dear Mrs. (surname) and Mrs. (surname)

Dear Mesdames (surname) and (surname)
                Both for women with different surnames

Dear Mesdames (surname)
                For women with the same surname

Ladies or Mesdames   *Simple but conservative*

TWO OR MORE UNMARRIED WOMEN

ADDRESS: Miss (name)
                Miss (name)
                mailing address and ZIP code

Misses (full name) and (full name)
mailing address and ZIP code

Misses (first names divided by commas) (surname)
mailing address and ZIP code
                For women with the same surname

SALUTATION: Dear Miss (surname) and Miss (surname)

Dear Misses (surname) and (surname)
                Both for women with different surnames

Dear Misses (surname)
                For women with the same surname

Ladies   *Simple but conservative*

GROUP OF TWO OR MORE MEN AND WOMEN

ADDRESS: Mr. / Mrs. / Ms. / Miss (name)
                Mr. / Mrs. / Ms. / Miss (name)
                mailing address and ZIP code

Messrs. (full name) and (full name)
Mesdames (full name) and (full name)
Ms. (full name) and (full name)
Misses (full name) and (full name)
mailing address and ZIP code

SALUTATION: Dear (courtesy title and surname 1) and
                        (courtesy title and surname 2)
                Dear Messrs. (surnames divided by commas)
                Mesdames (surnames divided by commas)
                Ms. (surnames divided by commas)
                Misses (surnames divided by commas)

(or use a style of corporate salutation listed in section 4.6)

Persons with Special Titles

In business and personal correspondence you are likely to encounter persons with special titles. Most of these individuals are listed in the charts in sections 5.2–5.5. However, you may run across special cases of multiple titles, degrees, or designations. Proper use of these special titles is simple if certain rules for use and order are kept in mind.

When using special titles, adhere to these rules of format:

1. Courtesy titles (*Mr./Mrs./Ms./Miss,* and plural forms) are usable with all other special titles except *Doctor* and *Professor.*

2. Title associated with a professional degree should not appear with an after-name listing of that degree. For example, you should use Doctor (name) or (name), M.D.

3. All titles and designations before the name should appear in the salutation as well as in the address, with the exception of *Honorable* or *Hon.* For example, a letter addressed:

> Professor (name)
> (Name of department)
> (Institution name)
> (Mailing address)

should bear the salutation:

> Dear Professor (name)

4. Degree designations and special titles used after an individual's name should never appear in the salutation. For example, a letter addressed:

> (full name), D.D.S.
> (mailing address)

should bear the salutation:

> Dear Dr. (name)

5. If multiple degrees or designations are to be used after an individual's name in the address or signature of a business letter, the titles should appear in the following order, separated by commas:

(full name), Jr., Senior, II, III, etc.
        religious orders
        theological degrees
        academic degrees
        honorary degrees
        position or post or professional designation

Below is a listing of the common special titles and designations most commonly found in business correspondence. The list is divided into two categories: titles that appear before, and titles that appear after the addressee's name. Note that you can use a plural form for multiple addressees with the same title.

SPECIAL TITLES AND DESIGNATIONS

Titles Before the Name	Titles After the Name
Doctor	M.D.
Dr.	D.D.S.
Doctors	D.V.M.
Drs. (plural)	Ph.D.
Honorable	Esquire
Hon.	Esq.
	Esquires (plural)
The Honorable Messrs.	Esqs.
The Honorable Mesdames (rarely used plural)	
Mrs.	
Madam/Madame	
Mesdames (plural)	
Mr.	Jr., Sr.,
	II, III, IV, etc.
	or
	2nd, 3rd, 4th, etc.
Messrs. (plural)	
Miss	
Misses (plural)	
Ms. (single or plural)	
Professor	
Doctor/Dr.	
Professors	
Doctors/Drs. (plural)	
The Reverend	
Rev.	
The Reverends	
Revs. (plural)	

5.2 MEMBERS OF THE CLERGY AND RELIGIOUS ORDERS

MEMBERS OF THE CLERGY AND RELIGIOUS ORDERS

ADDRESSEE	FORM OF ADDRESS	SALUTATION	COMPLIMENTARY CLOSING	ORAL OR WRITTEN REFERENCE
Catholic				
The Pope	His Holiness the Pope or His Holiness Pope (name) Vatican City, Italy	Your Holiness or Most Holy Father	Respectfully yours	Your Holiness or His Holiness
Cardinal	His Eminence (given name) Cardinal (surname) Archbishop of (diocese and postal address)	Your Eminence or Dear Cardinal (name)	Respectfully yours	Your (or) His Eminence or Cardinal (name)
Archbishop	The Most Reverend (name in full) Archbishop of (locality) (postal address)	Your Excellency	Respectfully yours	Your excellency
Bishop	The Most Reverend (name in full) Bishop of (locality) (postal address)	Your Excellency or Dear Bishop (name)	Respectfully yours	Bishop (name)
Monsignor (higher rank)	The Right Reverend Monsignor (name in full) (postal address)	Right Reverend Monsignor or Dear Monsignor	Respectfully yours	Monsignor (name)
Monsignor	The Very Reverend (name in full) (postal address)	Very Reverend Monsignor or Dear Monsignor	Respectfully	Monsignor (name)
Priest	The Reverend (name in full) (postal address)	Dear Father	Respectfully	Father (name)
Mother Superior	The Reverend Mother (name in full) (postal address)	Reverend Mother or Dear Mother	Respectfully	Reverend Mother
Sister	Sister (name in full) (postal address)	My dear Sister or Dear Sister	Respectfully	Sister (name)
Protestant				
Episcopal Bishop	The Right Reverend (name in full) Bishop of (locality) (postal address)	Right Reverend Sir or My dear Bishop	Respectfully	Bishop (name) or the Episcopal Bishop of (locality)

MEMBERS OF THE CLERGY AND RELIGIOUS ORDERS (cont.)

ADDRESSEE	FORM OF ADDRESS	SALUTATION	COMPLIMENTARY CLOSING	ORAL OR WRITTEN REFERENCE
Episcopal Dean	The Very Reverend (name in full) Dean of (locality) (postal address)	Very Reverend Sir or My dear Dean	Respectfully	Dean (name)
Methodist Bishop	The Reverend (name in full) Methodist Bishop of (locality) (postal address)	Reverend Sir or Dear Bishop	Respectfully	Bishop (surname)
Protestant Minister	The Reverend (name in full) (postal address)	Dear Sir or My dear Mr. (surname)	Respectfully	The Reverend (name) or Mr. (surname)
Mormon Bishop	Mr. (name in full) Church of Jesus Christ of Latter Day Saints (postal address)	Sir or Dear Mr. (surname)	Respectfully	Bishop (name)
Jewish Rabbi	Rabbi (name in full) or Dr. (name in full) (postal address)	Dear Sir/Madam My dear Rabbi or My dear Dr. (surname)	Respectfully	Rabbi (name) or Dr. (surname)

5.3 DIPLOMATIC AND PUBLIC OFFICIALS

DIPLOMATIC AND PUBLIC OFFICIALS

ADDRESSEE	FORM OF ADDRESS	SALUTATION	COMPLIMENTARY CLOSING	ORAL OR WRITTEN REFERENCE
International *Heads of State* Premier	His / Her Excellency (name), Premier of (name of nation)	Excellency or Dear Mr. / Madame Premier	Respectfully or Sincerely yours	Your excellency or The premier of (name of nation)
President	His / Her Excellency (name), President of (name of nation)	Excellency or Dear Mr. / Madame President	Respectfully or Sincerely yours	Your Excellency or President (name)
Prime Minister	His / Her Excellency (name), Prime Minister of (name of nation)	Excellency or Dear Mr. / Madame Prime Minister	Respectfully or Sincerely yours	Mr. / Madame Prime Minister or Prime Minister (name)
Diplomatic Officers Minister, American	The Honourable (name) Minister of the United States of America (postal address)	Sir / Madam or Dear Mr. / Madam Minister	Sincerely yours or Very truly yours	Mr. / Madame Minister or The United States Minister, (name)
Minister, Foreign	The Honourable (name) Minister of (name of nation) (postal address)	Sir / Madam or Dear Mr. / Madam Minister	Sincerely yours or Very truly yours	Mr. / Madame Minister or The Minister of (name)
Ambassador, American	The Honourable (name) Ambassador of the United States of America (postal address)	Sir / Madam or Dear Mr. / Madam Ambassador	Sincerely yours or Very truly yours	Mr. / Madame Ambassador, the Ambassador, or Ambassador (name)
Ambassador, foreign	His / Her Excellency (name), Ambassador of (name of nation) (postal address)	Excellency or Dear Mr. / Madame Ambassador	Respectfully or Sincerely yours	Mr. / Madame Ambassador, the Ambassador of (name of nation), or Ambassador (name)
Consuls, American	(name if known) Consul of the United States of America (postal address at consulate)	Sir / Madam or Dear (courtesy title and name)	Respectfully, Sincerely yours, or Very truly yours	Mr. / Mrs. / Ms. / Miss (name) or the United States Consul in (location)
Consuls, foreign	(Name if known) Consul of (name of nation) (postal address at consulate in U.S.)	Sir / Madam or Dear (courtesy title and name)	Respectfully, Sincerely yours, or Very truly yours	Mr. / Mrs. / Ms. / Miss (name) or the (name of nation) Consul in (location)

DIPLOMATIC AND PUBLIC OFFICIALS (cont.)

ADDRESSEE	FORM OF ADDRESS	SALUTATION	COMPLIMENTARY CLOSING	ORAL OR WRITTEN REFERENCE
Secretary General of the United Nations	His Excellency (name in full) Secretary General of the United Nations New York, New York 10016	Excellency or Dear Mr./Madam Secretary General or Dear (courtesy title and name)	Respectfully, Sincerely yours, or Very truly yours	Mr./Madame Secretary General or Mr./Mrs./Ms./Miss (name)
United States Representative to the United Nations	The Honourable (name in full) United States Representative to the United Nations New York, New York 10016	Sir/Madam or Dear (courtesy title and name)	Very truly yours or Sincerely yours	Mr./Mrs./Ms./Miss (name) or the United States Representative to the United Nations
Federal President of the United States	The President The White House Washington, D.C. 20500	Sir/Madam or Dear Mr./Mrs./Ms. President	Respectfully or Respectfully yours	Mr./Mrs./Ms./Miss President, President (name), or The President
Vice-President of the United States	The Honorable (name) Vice-President of the United States Washington, D.C. 20501	Sir/Madam or Dear Mr./Mrs./Ms. Vice-President	Very truly yours or Sincerely yours	Mr./Mrs./Ms./Miss Vice-President, Vice-President (name), or the Vice-President
President of the Senate	The Honorable (name) President of the Senate Washington, D.C. 20510	Sir/Madam or Dear Mr./Mrs./Ms. President	Very truly yours or Sincerely yours	Mr./Mrs./Ms./Miss President or (name), President of the Senate
President pro tempore of the Senate	The Honorable (name) President pro tempore of the Senate United States Senate Washington, D.C. 20510	Dear Sir/Madam, Dear Senator (name), or Dear Senator	Very truly yours or Sincerely yours	Mr./Mrs./Ms./Miss Senator, Senator, or the Senator
Senator	The Honorable (name) United States Senate Washington, D.C. 20510	Sir/Madam or Dear Senator (name)	Very truly yours or Sincerely yours	Senator (name), Senator, or the Senator
Speaker of the House of Representatives	The Honorable (name) Speaker of the House of Representatives Washington, D.C. 20515	Sir/Madam or Dear Mr./Madam Speaker	Very truly yours or Sincerely yours	Mr./Mrs./Ms./Miss Speaker or (name), Speaker of the House

DIPLOMATIC AND PUBLIC OFFICIALS (cont.)

ADDRESSEE	FORM OF ADDRESS	SALUTATION	COMPLIMENTARY CLOSING	ORAL OR WRITTEN REFERENCE
Representative to Congress	The Honorable (name) The House of Representatives Washington, D.C. 20515	Sir/Madam or Dear Representative (name)	Very truly yours or Sincerely yours	Mr./Mrs./Ms./Miss (name) or Congressman/ Congresswoman/ Congressperson (name)
Cabinet Officers	The Honorable (name) Secretary of (department) Washington, D.C. (ZIP code)	Sir/Madam or Dear Mr./Madam Secretary	Very truly yours or Sincerely yours	Mr./Madam Secretary, Secretary (name), or the Secretary of (department)
Chief Justice Supreme Court	The Honorable (name) Chief Justice of the United States The Supreme Court Washington, D.C. 20543	Sir/Madam or Dear Mr./Madam Chief Justice	Respectfully or Very truly yours	Mr./Madam Chief Justice, Chief Justice (name), or the Chief Justice
Associate Justice Supreme Court	The Honorable (name) Justice of the United States Supreme Court Washington, D.C. 20543	Sir/Madam, Dear Mr./Madam Justice, or Dear Justice (name)	Very truly yours or Sincerely yours	Justice (name), Mr./Madam Justice, or (name), associate justice of the Supreme Court
Federal Judge	The Honorable (name) Judge, United States District Court for the (district name) (postal address at court)	Sir/Madam or Dear Judge (name)	Very truly yours or Sincerely yours	Judge (name) or the Judge
Attorney General	The Honorable (name) Attorney General of the United States Washington, D.C. (ZIP code)	Sir/Madam or Dear Mr./Madam Attorney General	Very truly yours or Sincerely yours	Mr./Madam Attorney General or Attorney General (name)
District Attorney	The Honorable (name) District Attorney (postal address)	Dear Mr./Mrs./Ms./Miss (name)	Very truly yours or Sincerely yours	Mr./Mrs./Ms./Miss (name) or District Attorney (name)
State Governor	The Honorable (name) Governor of (state) (postal address)	Sir/Madam or Dear Governor (name)	Respectfully or Sincerely yours	Governor (name), Governor, or Governor (name) of (name of state)

DIPLOMATIC AND PUBLIC OFFICIALS (cont.)

ADDRESSEE	FORM OF ADDRESS	SALUTATION	COMPLIMENTARY CLOSING	ORAL OR WRITTEN REFERENCE
Lieutenant Governor	The Honorable (name) Lieutenant Governor of (state) (postal address)	Sir/Madam or Dear Mr./Mrs./Ms./Miss (name)	Respectfully or Sincerely yours	Mr./Mrs./Ms./Miss (name), Lieutenant Governor (name), or the Lieutenant Governor
Secretary of State	The Honorable (name) Secretary of State of (state) (postal address)	Sir/Madam or Dear Mr./Madam Secretary	Very truly yours or Sincerely yours	Mr./Mrs./Ms./Miss (name) or (name), Secretary of State of (state name)
State Senator	The Honorable (name) State Senator (postal address)	Sir/Madam or Dear Senator (name)	Very truly yours or Sincerely yours	Senator (name), the Senator, or Senator (name) from (district)
State Representative	The Honorable (name) State Representative or State Assemblyman/ Assemblywoman (postal address)	Sir/Madam or Dear Mr./Mrs./Ms./Miss (name)	Very truly yours or Sincerely yours	Mr./Mrs./Ms./Miss (name) or State Representative (name) from (district)
Chief Justice State Supreme Court	The Honorable (name) Chief Justice of the Supreme Court of (state) (postal address)	Sir/Madam or Dear Mr./Madam Chief Justice	Very truly yours or Sincerely yours	Mr./Madam Chief Justice or Chief Justice (name)
Associate Justice State Supreme Court	The Honorable (name) Justice of the Supreme Court of (state) (postal address)	Sir/Madam or Dear Justice (name)	Very truly yours or Sincerely yours	Justice (name), Mr./Madam Justice, or (name), associate justice of the (state) Supreme Court
Judge, State Court	The Honorable (name) Judge of the (state) Court (postal address)	Sir/Madam or Dear Judge (name)	Very truly yours or Sincerely yours	Judge (name) or Judge (name) of the (state) Court
Attorney General	The Honorable (name) Attorney General of the State of (state) (postal address)	Sir/Madam or Dear Mr./Madam Attorney General	Very truly yours or Sincerely yours	Mr./Madam Attorney General, Attorney General (name), or Mr./Mrs./Ms./Miss (name)

DIPLOMATIC AND PUBLIC OFFICIALS (cont.)

ADDRESSEE	FORM OF ADDRESS	SALUTATION	COMPLIMENTARY CLOSING	ORAL OR WRITTEN REFERENCE
Local or Municipal Mayor	The Honorable (name) Mayor of (city name) (city, state, ZIP code)	Sir / Madam or Dear Mayor (name)	Very truly yours or Sincerely yours	Mayor (name) or (name), Mayor of (city)
City Commissioner	The Honorable (name) Commissioner of (department name) (postal address)	Sir / Madam	Very truly yours or Sincerely yours	Mr. / Mrs. / Ms. / Miss (name) or (name), (title of post)
City Council Member	Councilman / Councilwoman (name) City Hall (city, state, ZIP code)	Dear Mr. / Mrs. / Ms. / Miss (name) or Dear Councilman / Councilwoman (name)	Sincerely or Very truly yours	Mr. / Mrs. / Ms. / Miss (name) or Councilman / Councilwoman (name)
Judge	The Honorable (name) Judge of the (court name) of (city name) (court postal address)	Sir / Madam or Dear Judge (name)	Sincerely or Very truly yours	Judge (name) or Judge (name) of the (court name) of (city name)
City Attorney	The Honorable (name) (title) for the city of (city name) (postal address)	Dear Mr. / Mrs. / Ms. / Miss (name)	Sincerely or Very truly yours	Mr. / Mrs. / Ms. / Miss (name)

5.4 SCHOOL OFFICIALS AND FACULTY

SCHOOL OFFICIALS AND FACULTY

ADDRESSEE	FORM OF ADDRESS	SALUTATION	COMPLIMENTARY CLOSING	ORAL OR WRITTEN REFERENCE
President (with Doctorate)	(name), (degree initials) President, (institution name) (postal address)	Dear Sir/Madam or Dear Dr. (name)	Very truly yours,	Dr. (name)
President (without Doctorate)	Mr./Ms. (name) President, (institution name) (postal address)	Dear Mr./Ms.	Very truly yours,	Mr./Ms.
Dean (with Doctorate)	(name), (degree initials) Dean, (school name) (institution name) (postal address)	Dear Dean (name) or Dear Dr. (name)	Sincerely yours,	Dr. (name)
Dean (without Doctorate)	Mr./Ms. (name) Dean, (school name) (institution name) (postal address)	Dear Dean (name) or Dear Mr./Ms.	Sincerely yours,	Mr./Ms.
Professor (with Doctorate)	(name), (degree initials) (name of department) (institution name) (postal address)	Dear Professor (name) or Dear Dr. (name)	Sincerely yours,	Dr. (name)
Professor (without Doctorate)	Professor (name) (name of department) (institution name) (postal address)	Dear Professor (name)	Sincerely yours,	Mr./Ms.
Associate Professor (with Doctorate)	(name), (degree initials) Associate (Assistant) Professor (name of department) (institution name) (postal address)	Dear Professor or Dear Dr. (name)	Sincerely yours,	Dr. (name)
Associate Professor (without Doctorate)	Mr./Ms. (name) Associate (Assistant) Professor (name of department) (institution name) (postal address)	Dear Professor	Sincerely yours,	Mr./Ms. (name)

SCHOOL OFFICIALS AND FACULTY (cont.)

ADDRESSEE	FORM OF ADDRESS	SALUTATION	COMPLIMENTARY CLOSING	ORAL OR WRITTEN REFERENCE
Instructor	Dr. (name) or Mr./Ms. (name) (name of department) (university name) (postal address)	Dear Dr. (name) or Dear Mr./Ms. (name)	Sincerely yours,	Dr. (name) or Mr./Ms. (name)
Superintendent of Schools	Dr. (name) or Mr./Ms. (name) Superintendent of Schools (school system name) (postal address)	My dear Dr. or My dear Mr./Ms.	Sincerely yours,	Dr. (name) or Mr./Ms. (name)
School Principal	Dr. (name) or Mr./Ms. (name) Principal of (school name) (postal address)	My dear Dr. or My dear Mr./Ms.	Sincerely yours,	Dr. (name) or Mr./Ms. (name)
Schoolteacher	Dr. (name) or Mr./Ms. (name) (name of school) (postal address)	Dear Dr. (name) Dear Mr./Ms. (name)	Sincerely yours,	Dr. (name) or Mr./Ms. (name)

5.5 MILITARY PERSONNEL

MILITARY PERSONNEL

ADDRESSEE	FORM OF ADDRESS	SALUTATION	COMPLIMENTARY CLOSING	ORAL OR WRITTEN REFERENCE
Air Force				
General Lieutenant General Major General Brigadier General	(rank) (name) USAF (military address)	Sir/Madam, Dear General, or Dear General (name)	Sincerely or Very truly yours	General (name)
Colonel Lieutenant Colonel	(rank) (name) USAF (military address)	Sir/Madam, Dear Colonel, or Dear Colonel (name)	Sincerely or Very truly yours	Colonel (name)
Major	(rank) (name) USAF (military address)	Sir/Madam, Dear Major, or Dear Major (name)	Sincerely or Very truly yours	Major (name)
Captain	(rank) (name) USAF (military address)	Dear Captain or Dear Captain (name)	Sincerely or Very truly yours	Captain (name)
First or Second Lieutenant	(rank) (name) USAF (military address)	Dear Lieutenant or Dear Lieutenant (name)	Sincerely or Very truly yours	Lieutenant (name)
Chief Warrant Officer Warrant Officer	(rank) (name) USAF (military address)	Dear Mr./Mrs./Ms./ Miss (name)	Sincerely or Very truly yours	Mr./Mrs./Ms./ Miss (name) or (rank) (name)
Chief Master Sergeant	(rank) (name) USAF (military address)	Dear Chief Master Sergeant or Dear Chief Master Sergeant (name)	Sincerely or Very truly yours	Sergeant (name)
Senior Master Sergeant	(rank) (name) USAF (military address)	Dear Senior Master Sergeant or Dear Senior Master Sergeant (name)	Sincerely or Very truly yours	Sergeant (name)
Master, Technical, or Staff Sergeant	(rank) (name) USAF (military address)	Dear (Master/ Technical/Staff) Sergeant or Dear Sergeant (name)	Sincerely or Very truly yours	Sergeant (name)
Sergeant	(rank) (name) USAF (military address)	Dear Sergeant or Dear Sergeant (name)	Sincerely or Very truly yours	Sergeant (name)

MILITARY PERSONNEL (cont.)

ADDRESSEE	FORM OF ADDRESS	SALUTATION	COMPLIMENTARY CLOSING	ORAL OR WRITTEN REFERENCE
Senior Airman	(rank) (name) USAF (military address)	Dear Senior Airman or Dear Senior Airman (name)	Sincerely or Very truly yours	Senior Airman (name)
Airman First Class Airman Airman Basic	(rank) (name) USAF (military address)	Dear Airman or Dear Airman (name)	Sincerely or Very truly yours	Airman (name)
Army General Lieutenant General Major General Brigadier General	(rank) (name) USA (military address)	Sir / Madam, Dear General, or Dear General (name)	Sincerely or Very truly yours	General (name)
Colonel Lieutenant Colonel	(rank) (name) USA (military address)	Sir / Madam, Dear Colonel, or Dear Colonel (name)	Sincerely or Very truly yours	Colonel (name)
Major	(rank) (name) USA (military address)	Sir / Madam, Dear Major, or Dear Major (name)	Sincerely or Very truly yours	Major (name)
Captain	(rank) (name) USA (military address)	Dear Captain or Dear Captain (name)	Sincerely or Very truly yours	Captain (name)
First or Second Lieutenant	(rank) (name) USA (military address)	Dear Lieutenant or Dear Lieutenant (name)	Sincerely or Very truly yours	Lieutenant (name)
Chief Warrant Officer Warrant Officer	(rank) (name) USA (military address)	Dear Mr. / Mrs. / Ms. / Miss (name)	Sincerely or Very truly yours	Mr. / Mrs. / Ms. / Miss (name) or (rank) (name)
Sergeant Major (all ranks)	(rank) (name) USA (military address)	Dear Sergeant Major or Dear Sergeant Major (name)	Sincerely yours or Very truly yours	Sergeant Major (name)
First, Master, or Platoon Sergeant	(rank) (name) USA (military address)	Dear First / Master / Platoon Sergeant or Dear Sergeant (name)	Sincerely or Very truly yours	Sergeant (name)
Sergeant First Class	(rank) (name) USA (military address)	Dear Sergeant First Class or Dear Sergeant First Class (name)	Sincerely or Very truly yours	Sergeant (name)

MILITARY PERSONNEL (cont.)

ADDRESSEE	FORM OF ADDRESS	SALUTATION	COMPLIMENTARY CLOSING	ORAL OR WRITTEN REFERENCE
Staff Sergeant	(rank) (name) USA (military address)	Dear Staff Sergeant or Dear Staff Sergeant (name)	Sincerely or Very truly yours	Sergeant (name)
Sergeant	(rank) (name) USA (military address)	Dear Sergeant or Dear Sergeant (name)	Sincerely or Very truly yours	Sergeant (name)
Specialist (all classes)	(rank) (name) USA (military address)	Dear Specialist or Dear Specialist (name)	Sincerely or Very truly yours	Specialist (name)
Corporal	(rank) (name) USA (military address)	Dear Corporal or Dear Corporal (name)	Sincerely or Very truly yours	Corporal (name)
Private First Class Private	(rank) (name) USA (military address)	Dear Private or Dear Private (name)	Sincerely or Very truly yours	Private (name)
Marine Corps General Lieutenant General Major General Brigadier General	(rank) (name) USMC (military address)	Sir/Madam, Dear General, or Dear General (name)	Sincerely or Very truly yours	General (name)
Colonel Lieutenant Colonel	(rank) (name) USMC (military address)	Sir/Madam, Dear Colonel, or Dear Colonel (name)	Sincerely or Very truly yours	Colonel (name)
Major	(rank) (name) USMC (military address)	Sir/Madam, Dear Major, or Dear Major (name)	Sincerely or Very truly yours	Major (name)
Captain	(rank) (name) USMC (military address)	Dear Captain or Dear Captain (name)	Sincerely or Very truly yours	Captain (name)
First or Second Lieutenant	(rank) (name) USMC (military address)	Dear Lieutenant or Dear Lieutenant (name)	Sincerely or Very truly yours	Lieutenant (name)
Chief Warrant Officer Warrant Officer	(rank) (name) USMC (military address)	Dear Mr./Mrs./Ms./ Miss (name)	Sincerely or Very truly yours	Mr./Mrs./Ms./ Miss (name) or (rank) (name)

MILITARY PERSONNEL (cont.)

ADDRESSEE	FORM OF ADDRESS	SALUTATION	COMPLIMENTARY CLOSING	ORAL OR WRITTEN REFERENCE
Sergeant Major	(rank) (name) USMC (military address)	Dear Sergeant Major or Dear Sergeant Major (name)	Sincerely or Very truly yours	Sergeant Major (name)
Master Gunnery Sergeant	(rank) (name) USMC (military address)	Dear Master Gunnery Sergeant or Dear Master Gunnery Sergeant (name)	Sincerely or Very truly yours	Sergeant (name)
Gunnery Sergeant	(rank) (name) USMC (military address)	Dear Gunnery Sergeant or Dear Gunnery Sergeant (name)	Sincerely or Very truly yours	Sergeant (name)
First, Master, or Staff Sergeant	(rank) (name) USMC (military address)	Dear (First / Master / Staff) Sergeant or Dear Sergeant (name)	Sincerely or Very truly yours	Sergeant (name)
Sergeant	(rank) (name) USMC (military address)	Dear Sergeant or Dear Sergeant (name)	Sincerely or Very truly yours	Sergeant (name)
Corporal Lance Corporal	(rank) (name) USMC (military address)	Dear Corporal or Dear Corporal (name)	Sincerely or Very truly yours	Corporal (name)
Private First Class, Private	(rank) (name) USMC (military address)	Dear Private or Dear Private (name)	Sincerely or Very truly yours	Private (name)
Navy and Coast Guard Admiral Vice Admiral Rear Admiral	(rank) (name) USN or USCG (military address)	Sir / Madam, Dear Admiral, or Dear Admiral (name)	Sincerely or Very truly yours	Admiral (name)
Captain	(rank) (name) USN or USCG (military address)	Dear Captain or Dear Captain (name)	Sincerely or Very truly yours	Captain (name)
Commander Lieutenant Commander	(rank) (name) USN or USCG (military address)	Dear Commander or Dear Commander (name)	Sincerely or Very truly yours	Commander (name) or Lieutenant Commander (name)
Lieutenant; Lieutenant, Junior Grade	(rank) (name) USN or USCG (military address)	Dear Lieutenant or Dear Lieutenant (name)	Sincerely or Very truly yours	Lieutenant (name) or Lieutenant (j.g.) (name)

MILITARY PERSONNEL (cont.)

ADDRESSEE	FORM OF ADDRESS	SALUTATION	COMPLIMENTARY CLOSING	ORAL OR WRITTEN REFERENCE
Ensign	(rank) (name) USN or USCG (military address)	Dear Ensign or Dear Ensign (name)	Sincerely or Very truly yours	Ensign (name)
Chief Warrant Officer Warrant Officer	(rank) (name) USN or USCG (military address)	Dear Mr./Mrs./Ms./ Miss (name)	Sincerely or Very truly yours	Mr./Mrs./Ms./ Miss (name) or (rank) (name)
Master or Senior Chief Petty Officer	(rank) (name) USN or USCG (military address)	Dear (Master or Senior) Chief Petty Officer or Dear (Master or Senior) Chief Petty Officer (name)	Sincerely or Very truly yours	Mr./Mrs./Ms./ Miss (name) or (Master or Senior) Chief Petty Officer (name)
Chief Petty Officer	(rank) (name) USN or USCG (military address)	Dear Chief Petty Officer or Dear Chief Petty Officer (name)	Sincerely or Very truly yours	Mr./Mrs./Ms./ Miss (name) or Chief Petty Officer (name)
Petty Officer (other classes)	(rank) (name) USN or USCG (military address)	Dear Petty Officer or Dear Petty Officer (name)	Sincerely or Very truly yours	Mr./Mrs./Ms./ Miss (name) or Petty Officer (name)
Seaman Seaman Apprentice Seaman Recruit	(rank) (name) USN or USCG (military address)	Dear Seaman or Dear Seaman (name)	Sincerely or Very truly yours	Seaman (name)

6

SENTENCE STRATEGY AND PARAGRAPH DEVELOPMENT

Successful writing of letters, reports, and memos requires knowledge of proper sentence structure and paragraph formation. Since everything you write will be in the form of paragraphs composed of individual sentences, you should know the general procedure for writing a correct sentence, rules for using rhetorical questions and emphasis, and strategy for building effective paragraphs. This chapter will serve as a guide for the formation and use of these essential components of modern writing.

6.1 SENTENCE LENGTH AND CONSTRUCTION

A sentence is a group of words that relates a thing *(subject)* with an action, state, or condition *(predicate)*. Sentences can be statements (*declarative* sentences), commands (*imperative* sentences), questions (*interrogative* sentences), or expressions of emotion (*exclamatory* sentences). Every sentence begins with a capital letter and ends with a punctuation mark. A sentence can be as simple as three words that stand alone as a complete, independent idea:

Ice is cold.

Or a sentence can contain many words, arranged in dependent and independent clauses:

He began with the belief that fundamental changes were needed to put things right, and that work within traditional groups was pointless.

When constructing a sentence, you should pay attention to good grammar, correct punctuation, and accepted construction rules.

This section is intended as a summary of the basic construction rules for sentences in modern business writing. Use the guidelines described below to improve the quality of your sentences.

Sentence Fragments

A *sentence fragment* is a group of words that lacks a subject or a predicate, or cannot stand alone to express a complete idea. Most sentence fragments remain undetected by writers because they are complete *phrases.* The sentence fragments below are phrases that contain modified subjects, but lack verbs:

Bathroom sinks, which are usually made of porcelain.
Shoes that are made of plastic.

You need to add an *action verb* applicable to the subject in order to make each phrase a complete sentence:

Bathroom sinks, which are usually made of porcelain, *chip very easily.*
Shoes that are made of plastic *often cost less.*

The sentence fragments below are *dependent clauses:*

While some young children need extra vitamins to stay healthy.
Since the peace treaty was signed.

You need to add an *independent clause* to each dependent clause to complete the idea and form a sentence:

While some young children need extra vitamins to stay healthy, *most children have diets adequate in these important nutrients.*
Since the peace treaty was signed, *the border between the two countries has been quiet.*

In general business writing, sentence fragments can be used in the following ways:

1. *Dialogue*—exact transcription of speech:

   "Here. Take it."
   "How old are you?" "Fifteen."

2. *Emphasis*—to dramatically stress a point or an action:

   It was fifty degrees below zero. Very cold.
   If there is a fire, close your door. Immediately.

3. *Transition*—discussion of ideas or directions for readers:

   Now our explanation.
   Illustration page 33.

Run-on Sentences

Run-on sentences are the exact opposite of fragments: they contain more than one individual idea or association of subject and action. Often run-on sentences are identified by the improper use of the conjunctions *and* or *but:*

Melissa's store sells wood-burning stoves and many accessories for coal stoves and installs new stoves but cannot deliver them because they have no trucks large enough for that purpose.

The remedy for run-ons is to divide the run-on into two or more sentences. You can choose a sentence length that fits your subject matter according to your personal taste:

> Melissa's store sells wood-burning stoves and many accessories for coal stoves. They also install new stoves, but cannot deliver them. Melissa doesn't have trucks large enough for that purpose.
>
> *or*
>
> Melissa's store sells wood-burning stoves. They also sell many accessories for coal stoves. They can install, but cannot deliver, new stoves. Melissa doesn't have trucks large enough for that purpose.

Pronoun Agreement

Pronouns substitute for or refer to nouns. You can make your writing easier to read by properly using pronouns. Instead of repeatedly using the name of the subject in a report, memo, or letter, you can use he/she, his/her, or him/her to refer to your subject. Pronouns must be used correctly in order to make sense. Since every pronoun refers to a specific noun you have clearly used before, the pronoun must *agree* with the noun's *number* and the noun's *gender*. This is called agreement of pronoun and antecedent (the thing that preceded the pronoun; that is, the subject).

Agreement in Number. Singular antecedents require singular pronouns; plural antecedents require plural pronouns:

> A *house* can be three rooms, but *it* is often much larger.
> Stationery *stores* sell paper, but *they* often are closed on Sunday afternoons.

Compound subjects are nouns that are joined by *and* or *or* and serve as the subject of a sentence. Compound subjects joined by *and* require plural pronouns:

> The *horse and* the *cow* went back to *their* dinners.
> The *manager and* the *owner* watched *their* team play.

Compound subjects composed of two or more singular nouns that are joined by *or* or *nor* require singular pronouns:

> The *manager* or the *owner* left *his/her* wallet.
> Neither *Mary* nor *Rebecca* will read *her* story.

Collective nouns are singular words that identify a group of more than one person or thing. If a collective noun (such as *team, pair, fleet,* or *committee*) is used to refer to a group as a single unit, then the noun requires a singular pronoun:

> The *team* went to *its* locker room.
> The *fleet* raised *its* sails.

If a collective noun is used to refer to individual members of a group, then the noun requires a plural pronoun:

> The *band* readied *their* instruments—flutes, clarinets, and drums.
> The *class* handed in *their* papers, essays on Napoleon.

Indefinite pronouns refer to antecedents that are not specific persons, places, or things. Thus indefinite pronouns are less exact in identifying subjects than other pronouns. Below is a list of indefinite pronouns and their intended number. Note that certain indefinite pronouns are either singular *or* plural; look further into the sentence to identify whether the pronoun needed should be singular or plural.

INDEFINITE PRONOUNS

SINGULAR	PLURAL	SINGULAR OR PLURAL
anybody, anyone, each, every, everyone, everybody, either, one, someone, somebody, nobody, neither	both many several few	all, any, more, most, none, some

Agreement in Gender. The gender (sex) of the pronoun must agree with the gender of the antecedent. These genders are either:

masculine (male)   —pronouns *him, he, his*
feminine (female)   —pronouns *she, her*
neuter (sex undetermined)—pronouns *it, its*

Masculine antecedents require masculine pronouns:

Mr. Grey watched closely as *his* father walked away.

Feminine antecedents require feminine pronouns:

While we waited, *Sally France* picked up *her* laundry.

Inanimate objects are neuter and require neuter pronouns:

We could not drive *the car* because *it* had a flat tire.

You must also differentiate between the words *who, that,* and *which* when they are used to refer to persons, animals, and inanimate objects. Use *who* or *that* to refer to persons:

Mr. Riley is a man *who* loves to play golf.
The *manager* is the official *that* called us together.

Use *that* or *which* to refer to animals and inanimate objects:

The *jewelry that* we sold was very beautiful.
The *horse* you ordered was one *which* we no longer own.

Shifts in Person, Gender, or Number. When using pronouns in sentences, try to avoid shifting from one person to another, changing the pronoun number, or switching the pronoun gender. Shifts such as these lead to confusion of readers due to improper pronoun references and overly complex sentence structures.

Avoid shifts in *person:*

During the years *I* lived with my parents, they expected *you* to eat dinner at home every night. *(Incorrect)*
During the years *I* lived with my parents, they expected *me* to eat dinner at home every night. *(Correct)*

Avoid shifts in *gender:*

The horse was stamping *its* feet, so I left *his* stall. *(Incorrect)*
The horse was stamping *his* feet, so I left *his* stall. *(Correct)*

Avoid shifts in number:

> *Neither* man got *his* ticket because *they* went to the box office too late. (Incorrect—*neither, his* are singular; *they* plural.)
> *Neither* man got *his* ticket because *each* went to the box office too late. (Correct)

Subject and Verb Agreement

In every sentence the verb must agree with the subject both in *person* and in *number*. *Person* refers to the subject of the sentence:

First Person—the person speaking (*I* or *we*)
Second Person—the person spoken to (*you*)
Third Person—the person spoken of (*he/she* or *they*) (*it*)

The form of the verb in every sentence is determined by the person of the subject and the tense of the verb. All forms of regular verbs within a tense are the same for all persons and numbers except third person singular, present tense, indicative mood; in this special case *s* or *es* is added to the base word.

PRESENT TENSE—INDICATIVE MOOD

PERSON	SINGULAR	PLURAL
First	I watch	We watch
Second	You watch	You watch
Third	He watches She watches It watches	They watch

Agreement in Number. Singular subjects require singular verb forms; plural subjects require plural verb forms:

> *A hat is* necessary when the weather is cold.
> *Shoes are* important for outdoor work.

Compound subjects require plural verb forms:

> *Automobiles and bicycles have* separate lanes.

Compound subjects composed of two or more singular subjects that are joined by *or* or *nor* require singular verbs. If the subjects joined by *or* or *nor* are of differing numbers, the verb agrees with the nearest subject:

> A *lamp* or a *candle helps* you see at night.
> A *lamp* or *candles help* you see at night.

In sentences containing both positive and negative subjects, the verb agrees with the number of the positive subject:

> The *skater,* not the *skiers, was* asked to give the speech.
> The *writers,* not the editor, *watch* the teletype for stories.

Words that are plural in form but name single subjects or ideas require singular verbs:

The *United States is* part of North America.
Politics is a frequent subject of discussion.

Subjects that are quantities or measurements are considered as singular in form if regarded as a unit:

Seventy-five years is a long time to wait.
One hundred dollars is a reasonable price for that table.

A collective noun (such as *team, pair, fleet,* or *committee*) requires a singular verb form if the noun is used to refer to a group as a single unit. If a collective noun is used to refer to individual members of a group, then the noun requires a plural verb:

The *committee works* late every night. (Singular)
The *team were* changing their uniforms. (Plural)

Indefinite pronouns refer to antecedents that can be singular or plural. The verb used with an indefinite pronoun must agree with the intended number of the indefinite pronoun; in cases where the indefinite pronoun can be of any number, look further into the sentence to see whether the verb form should be singular or plural. (See Table on page 65.)

The pronoun *you* always requires a plural verb form:

You are the person we need for the job.
You complete the work I give you faster than Bob does.

Proper Use of Modifiers

Words, phrases, or clauses that restrict or change the meanings of other words in sentences are called *modifiers.* When modifiers are improperly positioned or constructed, they can affect the wrong element within the sentence or destroy the sentence's intended meaning. Use the following list of common mistakes in using modifiers to improve your own writing.

Dangling Modifiers. Improper use of modifiers or phrases, called *dangling modifiers,* occurs when the word that the phrase should modify is missing or is buried within the sentence. A modifier may also dangle if it refers to an incorrect element within the sentence:

Smelling the fire, the window was opened by Bill. (Incorrect—*Bill,* the subject of the sentence, is hidden from the modifier *smelling the fire.*)
Sweeping and washing the carpet, the stains can be easily removed. (Incorrect—*Sweeping and washing* refers to *the stains,* not the correct subject of this sentence.)

In order to correct this problem, you can rewrite the sentence so that the word modified by the phrase immediately follows the phrase:

Smelling the fire, Bill opened the window.

Or you can rewrite the sentence to include the proper subject in a position where the subject can be clearly associated with the modifying phrase:

Sweeping and washing the carpet, you can easily remove the stains.

You can also write the sentence so that the modifier is last, in the form of a dependent clause:

> You can easily remove the stains by sweeping and washing the carpet.

Dangling Elliptical Clauses. A dependent clause (a group of words that cannot stand alone as a sentence) that modifies the subject of a sentence is called an *elliptical clause.* In an elliptical clause, some words are assumed rather than included—generally the subject of the sentence. If the elliptical clause refers to a different subject than the main part of the sentence, the phrase is a *dangling elliptical clause.*

> After helping the manager, the merchandise was all in order.
> (*Incorrect*—The merchandise clearly did not help the manager.)

In order to correct a dangling elliptical clause, you can rewrite the sentence so that the missing subject is within the clause.

> After *the clerk* helped the manager, the merchandise was all in order.

Or you can rewrite the main part of the sentence so that the subject of the sentence and the clause are the same:

> After helping the manager, the clerk saw that all the merchandise was in order.

Misplaced Modifiers. In order for your sentences to be understood by your readers, you should place the modifiers near the word or words being modified. You will find that your writing is clearer and less confusing if you place the modifiers correctly:

> Doctors use tools to check your breathing *called stethoscopes.* (Incorrect)
> Doctors use tools *called stethoscopes* to check your breathing. (Correct)

Be especially careful when using the words *only, almost,* and *nearly* as modifiers. Make sure you place these words immediately before the word or words they modify. Notice that the exact placement of these words can be crucial in determining the meaning of the sentences in which they are used:

> While I was at the restaurant, I *almost* lost twenty dollars. (Implies that person lost no money at all)
> While I was at the restaurant, I lost *almost* twenty dollars. (Implies that person lost some money, but less than twenty dollars)

Squinting Modifiers. When you use a modifier, make certain that it is clear which sentence element that word or phrase modifies. If a modifier is placed within a sentence so that it can affect either of two sentence elements, then that modifier is called a *squinting modifier.* In other words, readers cannot tell which way the modifier is looking:

> If you can get to the restaurant *right after three* you will get a free dinner.

In this sentence, the squinting modifier is the phrase *right after three.* This phrase could belong to the dependent clause:

> If you can get to the restaurant right after three . . .

This phrase could also belong to the independent clause:

> . . . right after three you will get a free dinner.

You have to determine which sentence element you intend to refer to with this modifier. One way to solve this problem is through *correct punctuation:*

> If you can get to the restaurant, *right after three* you will get a free dinner.
> *or*
> If you can get to the restaurant *right after three,* you will get a free dinner.

You can also rewrite the sentence to make the modifier's target plainer:

> If you can get to the restaurant, you will get a free dinner *right after three.*
> *or*
> You will get a free dinner if you get to the restaurant *right after three.*

Using Parallel Structure in Sentences

Effective writing sometimes involves communicating ideas that can best be expressed in complex sentences. When you need to construct sentences which contain multiple subjects, objects, or clauses, those sentence elements must be structured in the same manner. This system of sentence formation is called *parallel structure.* Parallel grammatical construction emphasizes parallel meaning to your readers.

The following sentences illustrate the uses of parallel structure for multiple sentence elements:

> A *car,* a *bicycle,* and a *motorcycle* were parked at the store. (nouns in parallel structure)
> Many children can *run, jump,* and *swim* better than adults. (verbs in parallel structure)
> Houses last longer if *windows are properly painted, walls are properly waterproofed, and floors are correctly finished.* (clauses in parallel structure)

Using Sentence Length for Effective Writing

The sentence length you choose is a matter of your own taste. You may choose to cover a topic in short, succinct sentences, or decide to use long, complex sentences to indicate the twists and turns of thought and logic. The way you organize your writing is up to you. But keep in mind these tips for effective use of long and short sentences:

1. *Short sentences* serve well to cover broad and involved topics. Your readers will find a report or letter composed of short sentences fast reading, clear, and emphatic.

2. *Long sentences* will give readers a sense of the complexity of your ideas or the necessity for further consideration of what you say.

3. *Juxtaposition* of long and short sentences in your writing can add emphasis by changing the rhythm of your speech. A series of long, involved sentences can climax in a short, powerful finishing statement.

6.2 RHETORICAL QUESTIONS

One strategy used by successful writers in order to focus their readers' attention on a specific issue mentioned in a letter or report is the *rhetorical question*. Rhetorical questions require no response from the reader. This type of question is an introduction to the writer's own opinions, a device to spotlight key issues about to be discussed, or a pointer to stress an important issue already covered.

Uses of Rhetorical Questions

As a Topic Statement. Sometimes a rhetorical question can be an effective topic statement. Not only does it ask a question which can then be answered in the author's own words, a rhetorical question gets the reader involved in considering the topic:

> *How do you go about buying a new house?* There are many ways to begin. First, you should decide on an area in which you would like to look. Then the logical step is to contact a real estate agent or broker who is aware of properties available in your preferred area. . . .

To Emphasize an Important Issue About to Be Discussed. Sometimes a general discussion of a topic needs a device that can focus the readers' attention on specific important ideas or concepts. A series of rhetorical questions at the beginning of a paragraph can make it clear what you consider the most significant points in the discussion that follows:

> *Is water pollution affecting our health*? Will the foreign matter in the water we drink affect our children? Can we easily avoid pollutants in our daily lives?

To Stress an Important Issue Already Discussed. After you have completed your discussion of an issue, you may choose to draw the reader's attention back to your central issue. Use a rhetorical question at the end of a paragraph in order to stress the theme underlying your discussion, or to raise an issue that shows how important your discussion really is:

> . . . which makes our brand of shoes the longest-wearing available for industrial use. And remember, we use only prime leather in *Super Duty* shoes. *So when your company needs new work shoes, will you buy an inferior product?*

Remember that rhetorical questions are special, powerful tools you can use to make your writing more effective. If you use them all the time, rhetorical questions lose their impact. Try to vary your writing style in order to maintain your readers' interest. If you use rhetorical questions sparingly, you will find that that they will enhance the effect your writing has on your business associates.

6.3 EMPHASIS

When writing a letter or a report, you will sometimes need to emphasize a point in your discussion. These points, ideas, or issues often fall in the middle of a lengthy paragraph or an involved line of reasoning.

Techniques of Emphasis

Use Rhetorical Questions. Rhetorical questions work well to indicate important issues. Place your question at the beginning of a paragraph to point out a central or vital issue.

Vary Your Sentence Length. A series of long sentences explaining an issue or idea can be ended by a short, concise sentence making a strong point. Not only does this clearly focus your reader's attention on a specific issue by isolating that issue, the variation of rhythm in your speech will stimulate interest.

Use Comments or Interjections to Disturb the Normal Flow of Discussion. By interrupting the customary smooth form of sentences, writers can call attention to words or phrases, or create special effects in writing. In modern, less formal business writing, this type of writing strategy is accepted as a useful method of emphasizing small elements in letters, reports, or memos. Look at the following examples of sentences without interjections or asides:

> I could get in contact with the chairperson.
> The reasons affecting our decision are many.

By using asides or interjections for emphasis, these sentences become much more forceful:

> I could, *if necessary,* get in contact with the chairperson.
> The reasons—*both public and private*—affecting our decision are many.

Use interrupting elements such as these carefully. Too many interjections or asides will disturb the reader and break an important chain of logical reasoning.

Reverse the Customary or Expected Sentence Order. Especially effective in discussions of complex issues is the technique of reversal of construction within a long sentence. Everyone tends to use a system of acceptable parallel construction throughout a letter or a report; reversing that structure within a sentence emphasizes a phrase or a clause because of its unique format. Look at the following sentence in a traditional parallel construction:

> These are the important qualities of a good school: adequate facilities, qualified teachers, and a concerned, involved administration.

In a reversed structure, this sentence is more emphatic:

> Adequate facilities, qualified teachers, and a concerned, involved administration—these are the important qualities of a good school.

If you use this method of emphasis, remember that it works well because it places sentences in a contrasting form from the usual prose style. Thus in order to preserve the effects of this writing tool, use it sparingly. This technique, when judiciously used, can add a spark of innovation to your writing style.

6.4 EFFECTIVE PARAGRAPHS

In order to convey meaning effectively in writing, you must organize your material into small units which serve as the basic structure for written communication—

paragraphs. Paragraphs are interlocking building blocks for the construction of discussions in letters, memos, and reports. By dividing the material to be covered into separate, individual units, the paragraph helps the writer to control a discussion. Yet paragraphs must coordinate with one another to stand together as a complete and interlocking whole. To create coherent communications, you must be able to master the techniques of construction within and transition between paragraphs.

There are four basic types of paragraphs: *introductory, developmental, transition,* and *closing.* While introductory, transition, and closing paragraphs all have a limited number of construction methods and aims, the developmental paragraph requires experience and knowledge in order to be effective. Since the developmental paragraph is the foundation of modern writing, you must be familiar with the construction methods and strategies when writing this type of paragraph.

Developmental Paragraphs

There are two basic types of developmental paragraphs: *argumentative*—used to convince or persuade the reader of the validity of an opinion or issue through data or facts—and *expository*—used to explain or describe a condition or event. You should be aware of these general paragraph categories so your developmental paragraphs have clear aims. Choose one type of developmental paragraph or modify it to suit your goals. When writing developmental paragraphs, follow a structured method and use accepted techniques within the paragraph.

Plan Your Method of Approach. Before starting to write, make up a thorough design for your paragraph. Select the subject or issue this paragraph will address. Limit the subject to a size which can be practically covered in a paragraph. If you find that you are trying to do too much in a single paragraph, divide the topic into two or more separate subjects to be treated in separate paragraphs. After specifying the topic, state it in a short, concise sentence. The *topic sentence* is the lead you will use in the paragraph to begin your discussion.

Collect the facts, opinions, and ideas you will use in the paragraph. Arrange these details in an effective order for discussion. Use one of the methods described in the section on development within the paragraph to organize your discussion in an effective manner. Finally, decide on your concluding sentence or sentences for this paragraph. Try to limit your conclusions to wrapping up the issues covered within the specific paragraph.

Develop Your Paragraph Effectively and Logically. A successful paragraph has a clear internal structure that develops an argument or an explanation. One method for internal development is the use of *movement* within the paragraph. The two kinds of movement are *sequential* (in order) or *expanding/contracting* (becoming more general or specific). Depending on the topic and your goals, you can choose any one of these methods:

Sequential Movement
1. Time order—arranging events or details in chronological order
2. Space order—arranging events or details in the order of *where* they appear (such as near to far)
3. Numerical/alphabetical order—arranging events or details in a list according to size, name, or number

Expanding/Contracting Movement

1. General to specific—arranging details or descriptions from the most general to the most specific
2. Specific to general—arranging details or descriptions from the most limited to the most universal
3. Least important to most important—arranging details in increasing order of significance
4. Most important to least important—arranging details in order of decreasing importance

You may also choose one of these other methods of organization within paragraphs for your own writing:

1. Comparison or contrast of facts, details, or opinions
2. Cause and effect of events and results
3. Definition of a topic or subject
4. Subdivision of a main topic into individual points

After you organize the details you have chosen to use in your paragraph according to a method of effective development, you can then begin to write your paragraph, moving smoothly and logically from point to point, detail to detail.

Use Smooth Transitions to Give Your Paragraph Coherent Structure.
You have to relate the separate elements in your paragraph in order for the development within that paragraph to make sense to readers. Move from one idea or thought to another by using *transitional words or phrases.* These are devices that relate issues through either indicating the relationship between the issues, or having readers make an association through stylistic similarities in your writing.

Conjunctions are single words that relate ideas or events. The common conjunctions are:

and   but   for   nor   or   yet

Each of these words can be used in the following way to relate separate issues:

and is used to show similarity between objects or ideas:

Swimming, running, *and* rowing are all difficult sports.

but is used to show differences between objects or ideas:

House-painting can be a difficult chore, *but* our new spraying machine will make it simple.

for and *yet* indicate a conditional relationship between elements:

Our feet had gotten cold, *for* we had been in the snow.
The food was still on the table, *yet* the guests had already left the party.

or is used to show a choice between objects or ideas:

I was going to mention the socks, pants, *or* shoes in this letter.

nor is used to show exclusion of an object or idea:

We have not gotten this package, *nor* have we received a refund.

Other words or phrases you can use for transition also indicate interrelationship between elements. These words and phrases include:

also	frequently	on the other hand
as a result	in general	recently
by contrast	in other words	similarly
in comparison	lately	thus
as a consequence	moreover	therefore
first	once	to be specific
for example	occasionally	usually

Other Techniques of Transition. These techniques rely on relation of elements through similar grammatical structure or the use of common grammatical elements. These techniques can include: repetition of subjects in consecutive phrases or sentences, repetition of key terms, and parallel sentence patterns within sentences and in consecutive sentences.

> We have come here to see a great *city*—a *city* of men, a *city* of women, a *city* of hopes and dreams.

Notice that the key word *city* draws together *men, women,* and *hopes and dreams* through repetition; the parallel structure of this sentence reinforces that relationship.

When your developmental paragraph is properly planned and smoothly executed, your readers will always get your message.

Introductory Paragraphs

Introductory paragraphs should present the subject to be discussed in a long letter or report and get the reader's attention. You can either list the major points to be discussed later, or introduce the central idea and conclusion without mentioning specific ideas used in developing your discussion.

Do not begin letters with complaints or apologies. Avoid unnecessary explanations and trite expressions. Be brief and succinct in your introduction. Readers will judge what is to come in a letter or a report by the quality of your introductory paragraph.

Paragraphs of Transition

Paragraphs of transition are short paragraphs (often one or two sentences) that connect two paragraphs or groups of paragraphs. The easiest and most effective way to construct a paragraph of transition is to mention the material covered in the preceding section, and to bring up the material to be covered in the following section in relation to the issue or issues already discussed. Use a conjunction or another type of word or phrase to relate the separate issues in the paragraph of transition.

Not all letters or reports require paragraphs of transition. Sometimes you will find that a simple sentence at the end of a paragraph is all that is necessary to lead into the following paragraph. You must judge whether a paragraph of transition is necessary and appropriate in order for your writing to be smooth and logically troublefree.

Closing Paragraphs

Closing paragraphs complete letters or reports. After a lengthy discussion of many issues, it is a wise idea to finish your treatment of the subject with a paragraph which collects your main points and emphasizes the purpose of the letter or report. Methods you can use in constructing closing paragraphs include:

1. Drawing conclusions from the material you have presented
2. Summarizing the preceding discussion
3. Re-emphasizing the central points of the preceding discussion
4. Making suggestions and suggesting solutions, if appropriate

Try to write closing paragraphs with the same qualities as your introductory paragraphs: clarity, brevity, and relevance. Remember that your closing paragraph is intended to reinforce your discussion, not weaken or diffuse it. Stay away from unnecessary details inserted as afterthoughts, remarks which detract from points made earlier, and trite expressions or cliches.

Similar to the paragraph of transition, the closing paragraph is an optional component of many short letters and reports. To determine whether a closing paragraph is necessary, read the letter or report and judge whether it seems to end abruptly. When a letter or report has no definite and final ending, consider adding a closing paragraph; a summary or a statement of your conclusions is usually effective and appropriate.

7

SAMPLE LETTERS FOR MODERN BUSINESS AND PERSONAL LIFE

Today's business, whether large or small, uses letters of many types on a regular basis. These letters may be inquiries, requests, orders, recommendations, or responses to the requests or orders from another business or individual.

Since so many individual types of letters are generated in the business community, you must be able to feel comfortable writing each of these different types of letters. This chapter will enable you to build most of the popular types of business letters from easily understandable forms and examples. Typical responses to these letters are also illustrated and explained.

7.1 SIMPLIFIED LETTER PLANNER

Most business letters use a common format. Chapters 2 through 4 explain these formats and their component parts. The only variables which distinguish most letters from one another are their purpose and content. Therefore you can do most of the planning and construction work on all of your business letters using one simplified form.

The Simplified Letter Planner on the following pages is the form you should use when beginning to write your business letters. This form will allow you to put together the parts of your letters which are commonly used in all business correspondence. After you use the Simplified Letter Planner, find the category of correspondence which best describes the letter you are writing. Use that section's Contents Planner to construct the text of your letter. Also use the appropriate example of your type of letter as a model for your writing, or as a model for your response to a certain type of business letter.

SIMPLIFIED LETTER PLANNER

Letter Format
The letter format I will use in the letter (such as Full Block, Block, Modified Semi-Block):

Heading
My complete mailing address (omit if letterhead stationery is to be used):

The date:

Inside Address
The name of the person or firm to whom I am writing:

The complete address:

Other information for mailing (such as department or branch):

Salutation
The salutation I will use in this letter is:

Contents
The purpose of this letter is (inquiry, order, adjustment, etc.):

Complimentary Closing
The complimentary closing I will use in this letter is:

Signature
The signature I will use in this letter is:

In the signature I will also include the following title or other identifying information:

Optional Letter Parts
The optional letter parts I will use in this letter and what they will say:

Reference Line:

Special Mailing and On-Arrival Notations:

Attention Line:

Subject Line:

Identification Initials:

Enclosure Lines:

Carbon Copy Distribution Notation:

Postscript:

7.2 LETTERS OF INQUIRY/REQUEST

Many business and personal letters ask for information or published materials such as catalogs or product brochures. These letters are all letters of inquiry or request. This type of letter is simple to write if certain key ideas are kept in mind.

Letters asking for favors or services must always be clear, specific, and especially appreciative of the reader's help. Make sure your request is reasonable and practical. Finally, be as brief as possible. Do not include useless information or explanations if they add nothing to the contents of your letter except extra length.

Compose the text for a letter of inquiry or request using the Simplified Letter Planner in section 7.1 and the Contents Planner below. Expand your entries on the Contents Planner into full sentences in your letter. Read the two sample letters and use them as guides for your own writing.

CONTENTS PLANNER—LETTER OF INQUIRY OR REQUEST

What I want:

The reason for my inquiry:

How the reader of the letter can help:

Additional information which can make my request clear and easier to satisfy:

Responding to the Letter of Inquiry/Request

Answers to letters requesting favors or services should always be courteous and prompt. If at all possible, grant the favor or request. In all cases, whether the reply is to grant the favor or to express your inability to do so, express your pleasure at the receipt of the request or inquiry. Always try to suggest additional or alternate sources of information for the correspondent. Finally, conclude your letter with an expression of friendly best wishes.

Compose the text for a letter replying to an inquiry or request using the Simplified Letter Planner in section 7.1 and the Contents Planner below. Expand your entries on the Contents Planner into full sentences in your letter. Read the two sample letters and use them as guides for your own writing.

CONTENTS PLANNER—REPLY TO A LETTER OF INQUIRY OR REQUEST

Can I fulfill the inquiry or request?

Why I can or cannot grant the favor or request:

The information or materials requested (if enclosed separately, be sure to say so):

Alternate or additional sources of information useful to the reader:

Any other suggestions which may help the reader:

LETTER OF INQUIRY—BLOCK FORMAT

ATLAS MOVING COMPANY INC.
Avon Drive
Charlotte, North Carolina 28222

February 23, 19__

Betts Tape Company
344 Commerce Drive
Pittsburgh, Pennsylvania 15219

Gentlemen:

As a company involved in short-distance moving of many small
businesses, we have used many types of packing tape. We are
currently trying to determine the best types of tape for our
work with plastic barrels.

Recently, we came across a small sample of your tape. It seemed
to fit the description of what we need for our work. In order
to determine its suitability we need full product information
on your line of tapes. Please send any samples which you feel
would be useful in our application.

Thank you for your prompt cooperation in this matter.

                              Sincerely,

                              Samuel Ewering, President

LETTER OF INQUIRY—MODIFIED SEMI-BLOCK FORMAT

56 West Auburn Street
Canton, Ohio 44705
January 20, 19__

Alpha Motor Company
455 Shaffer Road
New Haven, Connecticut 06525

Gentlemen:

I am currently working on a study of advanced design electric motors. For this project I need up-to-date information on the latest designs used in experimental motors.

Since you are the best-known producer of modern small electric motors, I would appreciate any printed materials you have available for your customers. Any suggestions which would aid my work on this subject would also be appreciated.

Thank you for your cooperation in this project.

Yours truly,

Sally Truding

REPLY TO LETTER OF INQUIRY—BLOCK FORMAT

BETTS TAPE COMPANY
344 Commerce Drive
Pittsburgh, Pennsylvania 15219

March 6, 19__

Atlas Moving Company Inc.
Avon Drive
Charlotte, North Carolina 28222

Attention: Mr. Samuel Ewering

Gentlemen:

Thank you for your letter of February 23 requesting information on our product line of packing tapes.

We would be pleased to send you complete information on the tapes we manufacture and samples of those tapes best suited to use on plastic barrels. In addition, I have enclosed our special pamphlet on tapes for special applications. See pages 37 to 50, "Packing the New Plastics," which includes helpful information on working with some of the newest packing materials and the latest advances in tapes for those applications.

You will receive the samples of our tapes by separate express mailing. I hope we can work together to meet your needs and expectations.

Sincerely,

James Davis
Director, Product Services

REPLY TO LETTER OF INQUIRY—FULL BLOCK FORMAT

Alpha Motor Company
455 Shaffer Road
New Haven, Connecticut 06525
(203) 393-2345

February 5, 19__

Sally Truding
56 West Auburn Street
Canton, Ohio 44705

Dear Ms. Truding:

I just received your letter of January 20 yesterday. Thank you for writing us and expressing your interest in our work.

At the present time, Alpha Motors is not engaged in any new developmental work on electric motors. Our specialty, gas turbine engines, is the bulk of our research effort. I really cannot furnish any information about electric motors which you would find useful.

I suggest you contact Continental Motors research department for the information you need. I think their work is closer to the topic you are researching.

Thank you for your inquiry. Good luck with your research.

Sincerely

Richard Thorn - Director of Marketing

7.3 SALES LETTERS

Businesses are always searching for effective ways of increasing sales. The sales letter, a specialized type of business correspondence, is just such a tool used by many organizations. Its aim is to convince readers to buy a product or service.

Successful sales letters have four specific qualities:

1. They get the reader's attention.
2. They stimulate the reader's interest in the product or service.
3. They convince the reader of a personal need for the product or service.
4. They convince the reader to immediately make arrangements to buy or use the product or service.

The mixture of these qualities in a business letter is the best recipe for success: the sale of your product or service.

Begin the effective sales letter with a device intended to attract your readers' attention. Questions, catchy sayings, cartoons, even jokes can be used to make readers want to continue reading the letter. Be sure to work in your product or service early in the letter. Appeal to the reader with some idea or issue that is universally important—making or saving money, home life, business success, or prestige. The first aim of your sales letter is to interest your readers in what you have to say and sell.

The heart of a good sales letter is the sincere and positive presentation of what you want the reader to buy. Emphasize the benefits the reader can expect from buying and using your product or service. It is best to be truthful and accurate about what you are selling, so be familiar with your product. You can cite the results of tests, offer guarantees, and even mention the responses from other satisfied customers in order to clearly and tactfully relate your product and its benefits to the customer. Use your knowledge of your readers to stress how your product will help them to achieve an important goal or realize a basic human desire.

Finally, the effective sales letter should motivate the reader to immediately purchase or make arrangements to purchase your product or service. The best way to ensure immediate response is to include with your letter: free return envelopes so the customer doesn't have to pay postage, simple order forms, business reply cards, and toll-free telephone numbers. Be sure to express your organization's eagerness to send more information, samples of your product, or even a salesperson to demonstrate the product or service. Make it clear that you appreciate the reader's interest and attention.

Compose the text for a sales letter using the Simplified Letter Planner in section 7.1 and the Contents Planner below. Expand your entries on the Contents Planner into full sentences in your letter. Read the two sample letters and use them as guides for your own writing.

CONTENTS PLANNER—SALES LETTER

In order to get the reader's attention at the beginning of the letter, I will:

What I am selling through this letter:

SALES LETTER—HANGING-INDENT FORMAT

Calamity Insurance Company   *Insurance Since 1879*

777 Riverside Avenue
Glendale, California 91201
(213) 240-1900

JAMES DOLE
Vice-President

                                        March 12, 19__

Ms. Sally Truding
56 West Auburn Street
Canton, Ohio 44705

Dear Ms. Truding:

Is your family financially secure? Will they have enough money
        to live comfortably if you were to pass away tomorrow?
        Make sure you are prepared for the worst!

Now is the time to start comprehensive life insurance coverage
        through the Calamity Insurance Multi-Adjustable policy.
        For just pennies a day you can assure your family of a
        steady income if you should pass away unexpectedly or
        be unable to work due to a serious accident.

The Multi-Adjustable policy is unique in the personal life in-
        surance market. Calamity guarantees cost-of-living increases
        in benefits payments to your survivors for the duration
        of the policy. Premiums are set according to your current
        age and the amount of coverage you wish to have. And at
        any time you can increase or decrease that amount of

SALES LETTER—HANGING-INDENT FORMAT (cont.)

Ms. Truding   -2-   March 12, 19__

    coverage simply by contacting us. Plus your policy
    accumulates cash value throughout its life.

Our thousands of satisfied customers prove the value of the
    Multi-Adjustable policy. James Arnow of San Francisco
    wrote us to say: "I shopped around a lot for good
    life insurance. Your Multi-Adjustable policy is the
    best buy in the business. How do you do it?" Sheila
    Dean of New York said: "I'm glad to be a member of
    the Calamity Family. One hundred years of experience
    behind me makes me feel secure. My low premiums
    make me feel terrific!"

Don't wait! Now is the time to join the Calamity Family!
    Fill out the enclosed business reply card and drop
    it in the nearest mail box. We'll send you full
    information on our full line of insurance, including
    facts on the Multi-Adjustable policy that thousands
    are now using. Act now and be certain of the security
    of your loved ones in the years to come.

                Cordially,

                James Dole

anf

Enclosure

SALES LETTER—BLOCK FORMAT

ATLAS MOVING COMPANY INC.
Avon Drive
Charlotte, North Carolina 28222

March 11, 19__

Harwood Pen Company
226 Main Street
Charlotte, North Carolina 28220

Gentlemen:

Do you plan on making a move? Transferring your headquarters
to a new location? Be sure you have the help you need!

Corporate moves are complicated business. Atlas Moving is the
corporate moving specialist with over fifty years of moving
Charlotte companies around town or around the world.

The North Carolina Business Society newsletter last year cited
our service as "the safest, most reliable" in the Charlotte
metropolitan region. And our "Fail-Safe Guarantee" is your
assurance of satisfaction.

Plan your move with us behind you. We offer full relocation
planning services which can start you on the right foot when
you start to plan your move. Call James Mosey at 704-252-3330
to find out about our full range of services and our economical
rates.

Remember, when planning to relocate, call Atlas. We carry the
world!

Cordially,

Samuel Ewering
President

This product or service can be described like this:

The reader will benefit from this product or service in the following ways:

Other things which will convince the reader of the quality and usefulness of the product or service are:

The reader can order the product or obtain more information by:

7.4 ORDER LETTERS

Individuals and organizations frequently purchase services and merchandise from firms in other parts of the nation or other parts of the world. Since it is impractical or impossible to make these purchases in person, these orders are made by telephone, telegram, or written direction. When these requests are in written form, they are called order letters.

Order letters are often no more than completed printed forms furnished by the seller for the convenience of the buyer. The use of a standardized form makes it simple for the seller of the product or service to make certain that the purchaser gives all necessary information for the purchase in an accurate, brief, and easily understood form. When no printed form is available for ordering, it becomes the buyer's responsibility to furnish that information in an order letter.

The essential contents of an order letter can be broken down into four important parts:

1. What is wanted
2. How it will be paid for
3. Where it is to be sent
4. How it is to be delivered

Effective order letters deal with each part simply, clearly, and completely.

1. Your request for the product or service must be as specific as possible in its description of what is wanted. Be sure to use the exact name of the item, the catalog or product number, if available, and any other identifying information. Remember to state the size, color, weight, or finish of the product, if applicable. Make sure you state the exact quantity of the product or service you are ordering.

2. Your order must include the price of each item, the total cost of the order, and your method of payment. Be certain your information is complete and accurate; most firms will not send out an order if there is doubt about payment for it.

3. Include exact data on where the delivery is to take place. Often merchandise arrives at the wrong place because the order letter neglects to mention a different shipping address. Do not depend on the heading of your order letter or the letterhead to provide the shipping address for the seller.

4. Specify the method of shipment for your order and how that shipment will be paid for. If a delivery is to be made c.o.d. (cash on delivery) specify whether

ORDER LETTER—FULL BLOCK FORMAT

Calamity Insurance Company

Insurance Since 1879

777 Riverside Avenue
Glendale, California 91201

(213) 240-1900

April 20, 19___

Harwood Pen Company
226 Main Street
Charlotte, North Carolina 28220

Gentlemen:

We wish to order the following items:

Quantity	Item	Finish	Unit cost	Total
50	#233 desk set	gold	$10 each	$500.00
25	#233 desk set	chrome	$8 each	$200.00
50	#707 pen	gold	$5 each	$250.00
25	#808 pen	chrome	$3 each	$ 75.00
			Total Cost:	$ 1025.00

Please send the merchandise out immediately via air express.
Our shipping address is the same as listed above, attention
James B. Poddle. Charge the merchandise to our account number
B-25295. Shipping will be paid c.o.d.

Thank you for your prompt response to our inquiries.

Sincerely,

James B. Poddle
Personnel Manager

ORDER LETTER—MODIFIED SEMI-BLOCK FORMAT

233 Main Street
Houston, Texas 77008
June 12, 19__

Williams Service Merchandise
535 Clinton Avenue
Milwaukee, Wisconsin 53223

Attention: Mail Order Department

Gentlemen:

Please send me by parcel post one set of your lifetime guaranteed six-piece screwdriver assortment. The catalog code, listed in the advertisement in the May Furniture Building magazine, is DD 003.

My mailing address is:

Canton Furniture
Box 34-T
General Post Office
Houston, Texas 77008

I am enclosing a check for the advertised price of $29.95 plus $3.00 shipping.

Very truly yours,

Robert Phillips

Enc.

the payment is for freight only or for the full amount of the bill. Shipment f.o.b. (free on board) includes the cost of delivery on the bill for the merchandise, either included in the price or as a separate item on the invoice. If delivery date is important, be sure to mention that in your letter. Do not hesitate to use the word "Rush" if you require the product immediately.

Replies to order letters are rarely necessary. Confirmation of receipt for orders (especially when the order is made by telephone) are most often simple printed forms or cards. If further information is necessary to complete the order, a letter of acknowledgment requesting more information can be sent to the buyer. Use a letter composition like those in section 7.7 to acknowledge an order and get more information, if needed.

Compose an order letter using the Simplified Letter Planner in section 7.1 and the Contents Planner below. Read the two sample letters and use them as guides for your own writing. Notice that you can construct an order letter just like a printed order form, or integrate your purchase request into the text of the letter. Choose the form which is most useful for your current order.

CONTENTS PLANNER—ORDER LETTER

I wish to order the following items:

Quantity	Item Name	Other Identification	Cost

I will pay for the items in the following manner:
(check, money order, charge account, c.o.d., or other)

Be sure to include complete information if using a commercial or personal account.

I want the merchandise delivered to the following address:

I want the merchandise shipped in the following manner:

Shipment will be paid by:

7.5 LETTERS REGARDING ACCOUNTS DUE

One of the largest continuing responsibilities for all business personnel is keeping the accounts of customers in good order. With the automation of most business accounting in recent years, the day-to-day billing of customers, receipt of payment, or correction of billing errors no longer has to be handled by general business persons. Yet there still are times when a personal business letter is necessary or desirable in order to properly deal with a matter of finances.

Letters regarding accounts due can be grouped into four categories:

1. Requests for payment
2. Letters of transmittal (accompanying payment)
3. Letters requesting correction of billing errors
4. Letters acknowledging billing errors or completed payment

It is important to be comfortable with the writing of all of these types of letters. Letters fitting the description of types three and four above are covered in sections 7.6 (Claim and Adjustment Letters) and 7.7 (Letters of Acknowledgment). When writing these types of letters regarding accounts due, use sections 7.6 and 7.7 for their construction details. Use this section and the accompanying Contents Planners to write effective letters requesting payment and letters of transmittal.

Letters requesting payment are usually not sent out until a bill is unpaid and monthly statements to a customer fail to elicit a response. Even though this type of letter can be very short and serious in tone, you should always be tactful and courteous to the addressee. Very often a nasty letter will make collection of an account more difficult and lose your organization a valued customer.

Collection letters range from polite inquiries about an unpaid balance to "last chance" letters mentioning other actions possible if the bill remains unpaid. Common to all requests for payment are three key elements: how much the customer owes the writer or the writer's firm, in what form payment is required, and what alternate arrangements can be made to pay the balance outstanding on the account. Be brief but thorough in your inclusion of each of these vital components in letters requesting payment for overdue accounts. It is also wise to thank the reader for his or her prompt attention to the matter you are writing about, no matter how insistent the tone of the letter.

Construct effective requests for payment using the Simplified Letter Planner in section 7.1 and the Contents Planner below. Expand your entries on the Contents Planner into full sentences in your letter. Be sure that the tone of your writing fits the situation you are writing about: first written requests for payment are generally pleasant inquiries; following communications can get more terse and to-the-point. Read the sample letters and use them as guides for your own writing at different stages of the collection process.

CONTENTS PLANNER—REQUESTS FOR PAYMENT

The customer owes the following amount for the listed account or merchandise:

Payment is required in the following manner by the following date:

Possible arrangements for payment in an alternate manner (such as installments):

Possible action which might be taken if payment is not sent:

Letters of Transmittal

Since most large businesses use machines to take care of routine billing and payment, the need for letters accompanying payments of accounts is quite small.

ACCOUNT DUE—FIRST REQUEST—BLOCK FORMAT

HARWOOD PEN COMPANY
The Best in Pens

226 MAIN STREET
CHARLOTTE, NORTH CAROLINA 28220

July 10, 19__

Robert Phillips
233 Main Street
Houston, Texas 77008

Dear Mr. Phillips:

Our records show that your account, #25295, has an unpaid
balance of $98.68. This balance is due to the purchases you
made from us in April and May of this year. Perhaps the
payment you made in May was intended to cover these purchases;
but those items did not come due until after you paid your
balance at that time.

Please send us a check or money order for this account at your
earliest convenience. If you have already mailed us payment,
please disregard this notice.

Thank you for your business and your prompt attention to this
matter.

Sincerely,

David Small
Credit Department

ACCOUNT DUE—SECOND REQUEST—BLOCK FORMAT

HARWOOD PEN COMPANY
**226 MAIN STREET
CHARLOTTE, NORTH CAROLINA 28220**

The Best in Pens

August 10, 19__

Robert Phillips
233 Main Street
Houston, Texas 77008

Dear Mr. Phillips:

We have not yet received a reply from you regarding the balance
due on your account #25295. We wrote you requesting payment
of $98.68 on July 10, and have been expecting you to be in
touch with us since that time.

If there is a problem with your making payment to us, please
let us know immediately. We can arrange a schedule for installment payments if this is suitable and convenient.

You can let us know about your account either by mail, or feel
free to call me at (704) 555-5432. Please contact us soon.

Sincerely,

David Small
Credit Department

ACCOUNT DUE—THIRD REQUEST—BLOCK FORMAT

HARWOOD PEN COMPANY　　　　　*The Best in Pens*

226 MAIN STREET
CHARLOTTE, NORTH CAROLINA 28220

September 10, 19__

Robert Phillips
233 Main Street
Houston, Texas 77008

Dear Mr. Phillips:

We are writing to you again requesting payment of $98.68 for
the balance due on your account. We have not received a reply
from you to our past letters.

Give this matter immediate attention. We look forward to your
cooperation.

Yours truly,

David Small
Credit Manager

ACCOUNT DUE—FINAL REQUEST—BLOCK FORMAT

HARWOOD PEN COMPANY

The Best in Pens

226 MAIN STREET
CHARLOTTE, NORTH CAROLINA 28220

October 10, 19__

Robert Phillips
233 Main Street
Houston, Texas 77008

Dear Mr. Phillips:

We have expected payment of $98.68 for the balance due on your
account #25295 for the past three months. You have not replied
to our letters requesting payment, either by phone or by mail.
We had hoped to simplify this payment for you by offering an
installment payment option; you obviously are not interested
in taking this opportunity.

We regret to inform you that unless payment in full is received
within ten business days, we will turn your account over to our
collection agency. Please send your check to us so this step
will not be necessary.

Sincerely yours,

David Small
Credit Manager

LETTER OF TRANSMITTAL—MODIFIED SEMI-BLOCK FORMAT

233 Main Street
Houston, Texas   77008
October 14, 19__

Harwood Pen Company
226 Main Street
Charlotte, North Carolina 28220

Attention: Mr. David Small - Credit Manager

Dear Mr. Small:

Thank you for your consideration in waiting so long for
me to settle the balance of my account #25295. I am sorry
that it has taken all this time for me to get in touch with
you on this matter.

I am enclosing a check for $50.00 to cover part of the
amount due at this time. As you mentioned in your previous
letter, an installment payment plan would be best for me to get
your firm the remaining balance. Could I pay the remaining
balance over the next six months? Please call me at (713) 555-2345
any time if there is any problem with this plan.

Again, thank you for your patience.

Sincerely,

Robert Phillips

LETTER OF TRANSMITTAL—MODIFIED SEMI-BLOCK FORMAT

56 West Auburn Street
Canton, Ohio 44705
July 30, 19__

Dr. Robert Millner
2 Old Quarry Road
Canton, Ohio 44718

Dear Dr. Millner:

I am enclosing a check for $45.00 as payment for your services as listed on the statement dated July 20.

Thank you for your help and kind attention in the last few difficult weeks. You have always assisted me and my family very well in the years we have been your patients.

Most cordially,

Sally Truding

Yet just as a letter requesting payment is occasionally necessary or appropriate, a personal letter of transmittal is sometimes desirable.

Letters of transmittal should be simple, short, and courteous. Such a letter should include the following data:

1. The amount paid
2. The method of payment (such as check, cash, or money order)
3. The number of your account
4. The date of the bill the balance is being paid upon, or its number, if undated

Be sure to include an expression of gratitude for the service or merchandise for which you are paying.

If a letter of transmittal is sent with either a partial payment or as a request for extended payment schedule, be sure to also include the above information. In addition, be certain to verify the exact terms under which you will be paying the outstanding balance of your account. Remember to thank the reader for the help and consideration given you in this matter.

Construct effective letters of transmittal using the Simplified Letter Planner in section 7.1 and the Contents Planner below. Expand your entries on the Contents Planner into full sentences in your letter. Read the sample letters and use them as guides for your own writing.

CONTENTS PLANNER—LETTER OF TRANSMITTAL

I am paying the following amount:

My method of payment is:

My account number is:

The date or number of the bill I received is:

If I am enclosing partial payment, the balance will be paid in the following manner:

7.6 CLAIM AND ADJUSTMENT LETTERS

When a problem arises in a modern business transaction, it is often most effective to deal with the problem in writing. A customer may complain about product quality, the delivery date, the service, or a billing error in a letter to an organization or a firm. These letters are called claim letters. The organization can respond to the claims of the customer, either by "making an adjustment" or refusing to do so. These replies are called adjustment letters.

Claim and adjustment letters can be the most difficult sort of business letters for you to write. There is no place for anger, bitterness, or sarcasm in a claim letter, no matter how upset you are by the problem you are writing about. You have to continue to show the reader of your complaint that you trust him or her to deal with your problem fairly, reasonably, and promptly. Antagonizing someone who you are asking for help will seldom result in the favorable action you want.

Writing letters adjusting complaints is equally difficult. Taking care of complex and sometimes confusing problems requires skill, patience, and tact. Remember that you are always responsible to be polite and businesslike to your customers. Be firm in the handling of the problems you see, but make it clear that you wish to keep the good will of your customers.

Claim Letters

Claim letters should be short, simple, factual, and always courteous. Three important elements must be included in the text of all letters requesting adjustments. These elements are:

1. The transaction about which you are writing
2. An explanation of the complaint or problem
3. What action you wish to take care of the difficulty

Data about each of these key parts of your letter should be complete and accurate. Include the date, the invoice number, the account number, the method of shipment, complete information on the merchandise ordered, and the quantity requested. Focus on the issue you consider most important, and make concrete suggestions about what you need done to solve the problem.

Construct effective claim letters using the Simplified Letter Planner in section 7.1 and the Contents Planner below. Expand your entries on the Contents Planner into full sentences in your letter. Be sure to double-check all information you use in your letter. Include an expression of appreciation for the investigation into your complaint. Read the two sample letters and use them as guides for your own writing.

CONTENTS PLANNER—CLAIM LETTERS

The transaction (sale, shipment, payment, bill, or service) I am writing about is (account number, bill number and date, product description, etc.):

The problem I have with the transaction is the following:

I want the company or organization to do the following in order to remedy the problem:

My suggestion for a remedy may be justified by:

Adjustment Letters

Adjustment letters should be short but informative, and courteous but firm. When writing an adjustment letter, be certain to include the following important elements:

1. Refer to the claim letter, identifying the transaction mentioned by the writer
2. State the action or adjustment which will be made
3. If practical, give the reasoning behind your decision

Respond to claim letters as promptly and as courteously as possible. Give complete information on the problem you are discussing. Try to be as fair and as cordial to the reader as you can; remember that the reader of your adjustment letter is likely to be upset by the problem he or she has written about. Good adjustment letters,

CLAIM LETTER—BLOCK FORMAT

```
                                        1600 Third Avenue
                                        Seattle, Washington 98101
                                        August 31, 19___


Williams Service Merchandise
535 Clinton Avenue
Milwaukee, Wisconsin 53223

Attention:  Customer Service Department


Gentlemen:

I recently ordered and received a set of wrenches from you,

AB 454 in your July catalogue.  I paid for these wrenches and

shipping c.o.d.

This set of wrenches is not at all suitable for what they were

intended.  All of them have defective jaws which do not close

properly.

I would like either a replacement set of wrenches or a refund

of my payment for them.  I believe that the high quality men-

tioned in your advertisements can also be found in many of

your products.  I hope this set of wrenches is one of those

products.

Thank you for your help with this problem.


                                        Sincerely,



                                        Carson Walker
```

CLAIM LETTER—SIMPLIFIED FORMAT

JAMES B. HARING FILMS

Industrial Filmmaking

2025 Kent Drive
Sarasota, Florida 33580

August 15, 19__

Continental Caterers
1000 Demarest Circle
Sarasota, Florida 33587

ERROR IN BILLING

Gentlemen, this letter is to notify you of an error in your
billing of our account. On the bill we have just received,
dated August 10, 19__, the balance as shown is incorrect.
We sent you a payment of $2000.00 on the balance for your
services on July 1. This payment was for the affair you catered
for us at the Sahara Bowl on June 15.

The correct balance on our account should therefore be the
amount you have listed on the current bill, $3545.00, less
our $2000.00 payment. We will, of course, pay that balance under
the usual terms.

Your service, as always, has been greatly valued by this company.
We send you our warmest best regards.

JAMES B. HARING - PRESIDENT

anf

cc Financial Auditing Department

ADJUSTMENT LETTER—FULL BLOCK FORMAT

WILLIAMS SERVICE MERCHANDISE
535 CLINTON AVENUE
MILWAUKEE, WISCONSIN 53225
(414) 535-9950

September 10, 19__

Mr. Carson Walker
1600 Third Avenue
Seattle, Washington 98101

Dear Mr. Walker:

SUBJECT: DEFECTIVE WRENCH SET

We just received the set of wrenches, catalogue number AB 454,
and your letter expressing your dissatisfaction with this set
of wrenches. In your letter dated August 31, you have requested
either a replacement set of wrenches, or a refund for the merchandise.

Our Customer Service department has inspected the set of wrenches
we received from you. They found that, as you determined, the
set of wrenches is defective. Apparently our supplier made a
mistake in their production.

In order to remedy this situation we are immediately sending
you a replacement set of wrenches. These wrenches have been
carefully inspected, and we believe that you will find them
to be of highest quality.

Please accept our apologies for the defective wrenches. We
appreciate your bringing our attention to this product.

Sincerely,

Paul Avery - Manager

ADJUSTMENT LETTER—BLOCK FORMAT

Continental Caterers
1000 Demarest Circle
Sarasota, Florida 33587

September 1, 19__

James B. Haring Films
2025 Kent Drive
Sarasota, Florida 33587

Gentlemen:

We have just completed an investigation into the billing discrepancy you mentioned in your letter of August 15. You claim that the payment made to us on July 1, in the amount of $2000.00 was to be applied to the expenses incurred at the affair we catered for you on June 15.

That payment, as our investigation determined, appeared on the statement dated July 10, 19__. The $2000.00 received by us was applied to your firm's outstanding balance.

We believe that upon a second check of your records you will find a record of our receipt of that payment. Therefore, the balance we list on the current statement is correct.

If you should find any other discrepancy on your account, please feel free to bring it to our attention.

Sincerely yours,

Ted Page
Head Bookkeeper

whether approving or denying adjustments, stimulate good will on the part of your customers.

Construct effective adjustment letters using the Simplified Letter Planner in section 7.1 and the Contents Planner below. Expand your entries on the Contents Planner into full sentences in your letter.

CONTENTS PLANNER—ADJUSTMENT LETTERS

I am writing about the customer's letter on the following transaction:

The problem with the transaction mentioned was:

The adjustment I or my firm will make is:

The reason for this adjustment (if practical):

7.7 LETTERS OF ACKNOWLEDGMENT

Many times in contemporary business it is necessary or polite to reply to a letter ordering merchandise, a letter of transmittal, or a letter pointing out a mistake in billing. These letters are called letters of general acknowledgment.

Letters of acknowledgment are seldom more than correspondence confirming the receipt of another letter, order, or payment. But this type of response is often the small element in modern business that means good business to customers. A thoughtful and prompt acknowledgment can be the deciding factor in closing an important transaction or obtaining a steady buyer for thousands of dollars of merchandise.

When additional information is necessary to complete a transaction, a letter of acknowledgment is also suitable. It is simple to add an inquiry about a key fact that is important to the filling of an order to a brief letter confirming the receipt of the order.

All letters of acknowledgment should be brief, informative, and appreciative. The specific function of this type of letter is to indicate to the reader that you received his or her letter and find it necessary and important to thank him or her for writing. Confirm the contents of an order or a payment in the text of your letter. Be sure to emphasize that you wish to be of continuing service to the reader. If necessary, ask for more information in order to complete your end of the business transaction.

Construct letters of acknowledgment using the Simplified Letter Planner in section 7.1 and the Contents Planner below. Expand your entries on the Contents Planner into full sentences in your letter. Read the sample letters and use them as guides for your own writing.

CONTENTS PLANNER—LETTERS OF ACKNOWLEDGMENT

I am acknowledging the customer's communication (include the date and order/invoice number) on the following transaction:

LETTER ACKNOWLEDGING PAYMENT—BLOCK FORMAT

BETTS TAPE COMPANY
344 Commerce Drive
Pittsburgh, Pennsylvania 15219

October 28, 19__

Atlas Moving Company, Inc.
Avon Drive
Charlotte, North Carolina 28222

Attention: Mr. Samuel Ewering

Dear Mr. Ewering:

Thank you for your payment and your letter of October 20. We are always pleased to hear personally from our new customers.

We would like to take this opportunity to thank you for your correspondence with us on the uses of our new plastic packing tapes. Your suggestions have been a great help to us in making our products useful to more customers.

At this time, Betts Tape is starting to market new packing barrels. We think you would be interested in this product for your own business. Read through the enclosed brochure. We'd like to have your comments on this new product.

Of course, feel free to contact us if we can be of service to you or your company in any way.

Cordially,

Richard Betts
President

Enclosure

LETTER ACKNOWLEDGING CLAIM—FULL BLOCK FORMAT

Dobbs Department Store　　　　　　　　　　　*Service Since 1890*

500 Cavalry Boulevard East
Canton, Ohio 44708

November 20, 19__

Ms. Sally Truding
56 West Auburn Street
Canton, Ohio 44705

Dear Ms. Truding:

We have just received your letter of November 16. In it you
point out an error in your last statement from us.

In order to determine whether this is in fact an error on our
part, we are currently beginning an investigation into the
apparent problem. This detailed examination of our records
will take at least a week to ten days. We will be in touch with
you regarding the results of this investigation at that time.

As one of our most valued customers, we hope that we have not
put you to any inconvenience due to the time needed for this
investigation. If there is any other way we may be of service
to you, please feel free to contact us by mail, phone, or
in person.

Sincerely yours,

Robert Earl
Customer Service Representative

LETTER ACKNOWLEDGING ORDER—BLOCK FORMAT

BETTS TAPE COMPANY
344 Commerce Drive
Pittsburgh, Pennsylvania 15219

October 28, 19__

Harwood Pen Company
226 Main Street
Charlotte, North Carolina 28220

Gentlemen:

Thank you for your order of October 15. We are immediately sending it out to you via private trucking as you requested.

We trust you will find the order complete and satisfactory.
Please let us know your reaction to our product.

If there is any way in the future Betts Tape can be of service,
be sure to let us know.

                              Sincerely yours,

                              Richard Betts
                              President

ACKNOWLEDGMENT OF REQUEST FOR CREDIT—BLOCK FORMAT

Haber Novelty Company
233 East 24 Street
New York, NY 10023

November 15, 19__

David Miller, President
Miller Toys
1500 Brooks Avenue
Richmond, Virginia 23220

Dear Mr. Miller:

Thank you for your letter of November 5. We are currently in
the process of checking into your request for a line of
credit with our company.

Due to the necessity of checking the references you have provided
with your letter, it will be two weeks before we are able to
give an answer for your request. We hope that you are not in-
convenienced by this period of investigation.

In the interim, we would like you to look at a full list of our
products. Enclosed is a catalog listing these products and their
prices. Note that a 10% discount is available on orders of
over 25 items.

We appreciate your inquiries. If there is any other assistance
which we may give you, please contact us.

Sincerely,

Francine Haber
President

Enclosures

ACKNOWLEDGMENT AND REQUEST FOR INFORMATION—BLOCK
FORMAT

Davidson Shoe Company   Fine Shoes for Men and Boys

P.O. Box 695
Lawrence, Kansas 66044

April 15, 19__

Mr. Alan Novick
23 North Seneca Street
Kansas City, Kansas 64105

Dear Mr. Novick:

We received your order and your check today. Thank you for
thinking of Davidson Shoes for your footwear needs.

In order to complete the packing of your merchandise, we need
some more information from you. You have on order two pairs
of our catalog number 795 BBA men's traditional slip-on
loafers. We need to know the colors you wish to order these
shoes in. They are available in tan, black, and brown. Please
write or call us, toll free, at (800) 233-3140 so we can complete your order and send it out quickly. Your order number
is 833-5095. Use this number when contacting us.

Again, thank you for ordering Davidson shoes. We think you'll
be happy with them for years to come.

Cordially,

J. Walter Riley
Customer Service

The action I or my firm is taking on this transaction is (investigating, shipping, crediting an account):

In order to complete this action, I need the following information from the customer:

Other ways I or my firm can be of service to the customer are:

7.8 LETTERS OF APPLICATION

Perhaps the single most important letter of your life may be the letter of application for a job. As the first form of contact between you and a prospective employer, the letter of application must stand as your representative for your business skills and personal integrity. The letter of application should be the ultimate in neatness, correct mechanics, and thoughtful construction.

There are two specific types of application letters. The first type is an answer to an advertisement for a position available for which you believe yourself to be qualified. The second type is a letter you write to a particular firm where you think there may be an opening available which fits your skills and interests. In both cases, the strategy best used in writing a letter of application is the same.

The strategy for writing a successful letter of application has three separate components: a clear statement of the purpose of the letter, concise and accurate background information on the applicant, and a request for an interview with the company. The letter of application can either contain the important background information within the message of the letter, or serve as a cover letter for a separate data sheet, or "résumé." Both methods of writing letters of application follow the strategy mentioned above; it is up to you to choose the approach which suits you best.

Purpose of the Letter

Always state in the first paragraph of a letter of application that you are applying for a job. Explain where you saw the job advertised, if that is applicable. Whenever possible apply for a specific position, rather than a general opening. Try to briefly give a reason why you want the job.

Background Information

Contained in Letter. When background information important to your application is integrated into the text of the letter, be sure to be thorough and complete. The information you should provide falls into three general categories: personal data, education, and work experience.

In the personal data section you should include: age, height and weight, condition of health, marital status, and complete address. The inclusion of telephone and Social Security numbers is optional. Include all information that is necessary for your consideration for the job.

Educational background should cover from high school to the present. In this section you should include: the name and address of the school, the dates attended, your graduation date and concentration, other fields of emphasis, awards, and important activities. Mention courses or activities that are especially relevant to your qualifications for employment. It is best to list the most recent educational experience first, and work back in time.

List your work experience, beginning with your most recent or present position. In this section you should include: the dates of your employment, your specific duties and responsibilities, and the complete address of the firm or organization. You may also choose to list the name of your immediate supervisor. Jobs that add to your suitability for prospective employment are most important and should be emphasized.

Finally, in the reference section it is advisable to list three or more individuals who can attest to your ability and character. State how you know the individuals, and give their complete addresses. Be sure to ask these people for permission to use their names, and make sure they would be willing to write a letter of recommendation for you if requested. If you choose not to list references on your first communication with a prospective employer, note that references are available upon request.

Use the sample résumé as an illustration of what information you might include in the text of your letter. Organize your information clearly and neatly. The *Letter of Application Without Résumé* is a good example of an attractive presentation of data within the body of a letter of application.

Contained on Résumé. When you enclose a separate résumé with a letter of application, the letter of application becomes a useful way to emphasize the most pertinent information listed on the data sheet. Since full information about you is contained on the résumé enclosed with the letter, use the section on background information in the text of the letter to point out qualities which make you uniquely qualified for the job.

Use of a separate résumé can make a letter of application shorter, clearer, and more visually attractive. If you choose to use this method of presentation, remember to mention in your cover letter that a separate résumé is included. Make the proper "enclosure" notation at the end of the cover letter.

The Interview Request

The final paragraph of any letter of application should contain a request for an interview at the convenience of the organization to whom you are applying. If there are any restrictions as to the time or date you could attend an interview, state those restrictions and the reason for them. Tell the company how, when, and where you can be reached to set a date for the interview.

Although a résumé is not necessary for a successful letter of application, it can be a useful tool in the application process for any job. It is a wise idea to have a current personal résumé available whenever considering a career move. Style for a résumé is largely a matter of personal choice. A résumé must be neat, clear, and attractive. Any extra touches you might choose to add to your résumé are up to you; you might include a sample of your writing, artwork, or a photograph. Make sure the résumé is professionally reproduced on high-quality paper and includes all your "vital statistics." An effective example of the basic résumé accompanies the *Letter of Application With Separate Résumé*.

Construct effective letters of application using the Simplified Letter Planner in section 7.1 and the Contents Planner below. Make sure that the résumé is neat and emphasizes important facts relevant to your application. Read the sample letters and the résumé and use them as guides for your own writing.

CONTENTS PLANNER—LETTER OF APPLICATION

Purpose of the Letter

I am applying for the following position:

I found out about the available job through:

The reason I would like the job:

Background Information

If I am enclosing a résumé, I will say so in the following way:

(Complete the following sections if no résumé is included.)

*Personal Data:
    Age:
    Height:
    Weight:
    Health:
    Marital status:
    Permanent address:
    Other pertinent information:

*Education:
    Graduate School: (name)   (address)

    Dates attended: Degree awarded:

    Field of Concentration:

    Awards and special activities:

    College: (name)   (address)

    Dates attended: Degree awarded:

    Field of Concentration:

Awards and special activities:

High School: (name)   (address)

Dates attended: Date of graduation:

Areas I specialized in:

Awards and special activities:

*Work Experience relevant to the job I am seeking:
        (List jobs, beginning with the most recent, or present)

Dates of Employment	Job Title	Company Name and Address	My duties and responsibilities

*References:

The following (three or more) people can be contacted as to my character and
    qualifications (If you do not supply names, then say that references are avail-
    able upon request.):

Full name	Addresses and/or telephone #	How we are associated

The Interview Request
I would like an interview with a representative of the company. Restrictions of time
or date are:
I cannot attend an interview because:

I can be reached to arrange the time and place of an interview by:

Times I can best be reached are:

Acknowledging Letters of Application

Although all applications for employment do not require a written acknowledgment, it is a courtesy to do so. Of course, you should send an acknowledgment to
any applicant whom you wish to consider for immediate or future employment. In all
cases, it is simple to write a basic acknowledgment to an applicant for employment.

LETTER OF APPLICATION WITHOUT RÉSUMÉ—FULL BLOCK FORMAT

56 Lakeside Avenue
Verona, New Jersey 07044
November 25, 19___

Newtown Construction Company
445 Oak Street
Weston, Connecticut 06880

Attention: Mr. George Billings

Dear Mr. Billings:

I would like to apply for the position of Assistant Construction
Engineer with Newtown Construction. This letter is in response
to your advertisement in the New York Times classified section
of November 20. I think my qualifications for this job are
excellent, and that I can be an advantage to a company with the
fine reputation of Newtown Construction.

I am currently employed as a construction coordinator with North
Jersey Construction, Inc. I joined them two years ago, and
have been in charge of residential planning for them since I
joined the company. Before that I was a planning engineer for
the city of New Paltz, New York, for three years. My responsibilities included the Thomas Hart urban redevelopment project
completed this year.

My training included three years at the Urban Planning Institute
for which I received my doctorate in architecture and urban
planning in June, 19___. My undergraduate work was done in
architecture at the University of Ohio from 19___ to 19___. I
graduated Magna Cum Laude in May, 19___.

LETTER OF APPLICATION WITHOUT RÉSUMÉ—FULL BLOCK FORMAT
(cont.)

Mr. Billings
Page 2
November 25, 19__

Currently I am 33 years of age, 5 feet 11 inches in height, and weigh 165 pounds. I am single, and in excellent health.

My permanent address is listed above, but I would be willing to relocate if the position you have available requires that I do so.

If you desire to contact my present employer for a recommendation, ask for my supervisor, Mr. Donald McGuire. His telephone number is (201) 239-6837. I am certain that he would be pleased to discuss my contribution to North Jersey Construction with you. I will supply other references, if you require them, upon request.

I would be pleased to cover any additional material with you in a personal interview at your convenience. Although I am currently engaged in a project that takes me out of town on Tuesdays and Fridays, I can be reached at (201) 239-6830 during business hours on all other days.

I am eager to hear from you about this position.

Sincerely yours,

Ralph Millman

LETTER OF APPLICATION WITHOUT RESUME—BLOCK FORMAT

```
                              4950 West 105 Street
                              Chicago, Illinois 60611
                              April 23, 19__


Keller Advertising Agency
160 East Grand Avenue
Chicago, Illinois 60603

Attention:  Personnel Department


Gentlemen:

As a major advertising agency in central Chicago, your company
has been recommended to me as a firm which could use an
experienced word processor.  I would like to apply for a
position with Keller Advertising as a secretary-word processor.
My qualifications are as follows:

     Graduate of Central High School, Chicago, June 19__.
Trained in word processing at Hobbs Institute, Chicago,
January to August 19__.

     Current employer:  Nevins Associates, 2203 Michigan,
Chicago.  Word processing secretary for four years.  My
supervisor is Mr. Edward Nevins.  His phone number is
964-4233.

     Past employer:  City of Chicago, Municipal Hall, Chicago.
Secretary to the Mayor 19__ to 19__.

     I am 34 years old, single, and in excellent health.

You are welcome to contact my past and present employers for
references.  Other references, if required, will be available
upon request.

I would be pleased to have a personal interview with a
representative of your company.  You can contact me at
964-4200 on business days.  I look forward to personally
discussing my unique qualifications for a position with
Keller Advertising.


                         Sincerely,



                         David Norton
```

LETTER OF APPLICATION WITH SEPARATE RÉSUMÉ—BLOCK FORMAT

```
                                        99 Willow Street
                                        Brooklyn, New York 11201
                                        September 1, 19__


Phillips, McCann, and Frost Associates
33 Wall Street
New York, New York 10003

Attention:  Personnel Department

Gentlemen:

Through Bernard Warren, whose firm of Warren Associates is a
customer of yours, I have learned of your exceptional training
program in the Securities Trading market.  I feel that with my
experience and training you would find me to be a fine
addition to your staff, and a candidate for this training
program.  I would like to enter this field with a company like
Phillips, McCann, and Frost because of your excellent reputation
for honesty and accuracy.

I am enclosing a copy of my current resume.  Please note the
following data:

    1.  My college training specialized in economics.

    2.  The bulk of my work experience has included financial
        planning and supervision of employees.

If you feel that my qualifications meet your requirements, I
would appreciate an interview with a representative of your
company at your convenience.

Thank you for your consideration.


                                        Sincerely,



                                        Roberta Dearing


Enclosure
```

<u>RESUME</u>

<u>Roberta Dearing</u>

<u>Personal</u>:

   <u>Birthdate</u>:   July 10, 19__   New York City

   <u>Address</u>:   99 Willow Street
                                      Brooklyn, New York 11201
                                      (212) 835-8802

   <u>Health</u>:'   Excellent   <u>Social Security</u>:000-00-0000

<u>Education</u>:

   <u>College</u>:   Dean University
                      Providence, Rhode Island 02912
                      September 19__ to June 19__

     Awarded B.A. degree in Economics, minor in Education.

   <u>High School</u>:   Susan B. Wagner High School
                      Staten Island, New York

     Graduated in June, 19__. Specialties: Mathematics, History.

<u>Job Objective</u>: Operations management in the Financial/Securities
                 trading market, emphasis on trading and account
                 supervision.

<u>Employment Experience</u>:

August 19__ - Present   <u>Auditor</u>, Gimbels New York. Supervised
                            overall procedural and financial auditing
                            for the retail operation.

March 19__ - July 19__   <u>Operations Manager</u>, Gimbels East,
New York. Supervised complete store
activity including financial, ordering,
and personnel. 19__ gross receipts
totalled over 3.2 million dollars.

October 19__ - March 19__   <u>Restaurant Manager</u>, Gimbels New York.
Supervised all aspects of restaurant with
19__ gross receipts over 1.1 million
dollars.

<u>Hobbies</u>: Skiing, Tennis, Squash

<u>References</u>: Available upon request.

The three types of acknowledgment letters that you might have to write are:

1. Letter that expresses your desire to interview the applicant for a position

2. Letter that thanks the applicant for applying for the position and informs him or her that the application will be given future consideration

3. Letter that thanks the applicant for applying but expresses your regret that no position is available or suitable for the applicant

Each of these varieties of acknowledgment should be brief and to the point. If you wish to interview the applicant, suggest a time, a date, and a place subject to confirmation by the applicant. When you wish to keep the applicant's file for possible future use, be sure to let the applicant know that you may be in contact with him or her at a later date.

Send your letter of acknowledgment promptly upon receipt of an application. Remember to be courteous but firm in your writing style.

Read the sample letters, which illustrate the three types of acknowledgment for the receipt of employment applications, and use them as guides for your own writing. Note that because of its short length, the acknowledgment of this type is quite suited to the half-sheet format.

Applicant Follow-Up Letters

After you have submitted an application for employment, you may wish to follow it with another, brief letter. This "follow-up" letter can take three forms:

1. Inquiry into the status of your application, if you have received no acknowledgment of its receipt

2. Affirmation of your desire to be considered for a future position, if one is currently not available

3. Letter expressing your appreciation after a personal interview

A letter of inquiry should be written after two weeks from the date of your application, if you have not received an acknowledgment of its receipt and you desire to be seriously considered for a position. Your note should be courteous and brief. Be sure to mention the date of your application, the position you have applied for, and your belief that you are qualified for the position for which you applied. End your letter with a request for information on the current status of your application. Remember to thank the reader for the help you are requesting.

After you receive a letter which offers no immediate employment, but does offer the consideration for a future job, decide whether or not you wish to be seriously considered for future employment by that company. If so, write a note of appreciation that thanks the writer of the letter who acknowledged your application. Stress your interest in the possible availability of future jobs with the company, and your hope that when a position becomes available, your application will be considered favorably.

If a company should grant you an interview as part of the application process, it is wise to follow that interview with a letter of appreciation. Express your thanks for the considerations extended to you during your visit, and your enjoyment of the conversation you had with a representative of the company. Mention again your interest in the position for which you are being considered. Close your note with a

LETTER OF ACKNOWLEDGMENT OF APPLICATION—BLOCK FORMAT

NEWTOWN CONSTRUCTION COMPANY   *SINCE 1955*
445 OAK STREET
WESTON, CONNECTICUT 06880

December 1, 19__

Mr. Ralph Millman
56 Lakeside Avenue
Verona, New Jersey 07044

Dear Mr. Millman:

Thank you for your letter of November 25 applying for the
position of Assistant Construction Engineer. I received your
letter today, and read it with great interest.

We would like to meet and talk with you about your application.
Please come to our office on Wednesday, December 15, at 2:00
p.m. Mr. Freeman in our personnel office will be waiting for
your arrival.

If this time and date are inconvenient for you, please call
me at (203) 999-2300 and we will set another date for your
interview.

Cordially,

George Billings
Director of Personnel

LETTER OF ACKNOWLEDGMENT OF APPLICATION—HALF-SHEET
FORMAT

Keller Advertising Agency
160 East Grand Avenue
Chicago, Illinois 60603

March 1, 19___

Mr. David Norton
4950 West 105 Street
Chicago, Illinois 60611

Dear Mr. Norton:

Thank you for your application of April 23.

Due to our current staffing situation, we are

not currently hiring personnel with your qual-

ifications.

We would like to keep your application in our

active file for future consideration. If an

opening should appear for someone with your

fine qualifications, we will contact you at

that time.

Sincerely,

Sara Walker
Personnel

LETTER OF ACKNOWLEDGMENT OF APPLICATION—HALF-SHEET FORMAT

Phillips, McCann, and Frost Associates
33 Wall Street
New York, New York 10003

September 15, 19__

Ms. Roberta Dearing
99 Willow Street
Brooklyn, New York 11201

Dear Ms. Dearing:

Thank you for your letter of September 1.

We read your letter with great interest.

Unfortunately, you do not meet the quali-

fications we normally expect for entry

into our training program.

Again, thank you for writing us. We wish

you the best of luck in your career.

Sincerely,

Samuel Sloane
Personnel

---

brief thanks and the hope that you will soon hear from the company about your application.

Read the sample letters, which illustrate the three different varieties of applicant follow-up letters, and use them as guides. You should model your own writing after the one which most closely fits your own uses.

APPLICANT FOLLOW-UP LETTER—FULL BLOCK FORMAT

56 Lakeside Avenue
Verona, New Jersey 07044
December 16, 19__

Mr. George Billings
Director of Personnel
Newtown Construction Company
445 Oak Street
Weston, Connecticut 06880

Dear Mr. Billings:

It was a great pleasure to meet you yesterday, and discuss

with you and Mr. Freeman my application to Newtown Construction.

I especially appreciated your presentation on the new residen-

tial planning philosophy initiated by your company. This sort

of innovative approach to planning is of great personal interest

to me.

I believe that I could contribute greatly to a company like

Newtown Construction. The emphasis on modern solutions to

complex construction problems is very much part of my working

style as well as your company's.

I hope to hear from you soon.

Sincerely,

Ralph Millman

APPLICANT FOLLOW-UP LETTER—BLOCK FORMAT

4950 West 105 Street
Chicago, Illinois 60611
March 8, 19__

Ms. Sara Walker - Personnel
Keller Advertising Agency
160 East Grand Avenue
Chicago, Illinois 60603

Dear Ms. Walker:

Thank you for the kind response to my letter of application.
I regret that your company does not currently have a position
for someone of my qualifications.

I am still greatly interested in the possibility of employment
with the Keller Advertising Agency. Please keep my application
on hand in case a position should become available.

I look forward to hearing from you in the future.

Sincerely,

David Norton

APPLICANT FOLLOW-UP LETTER—BLOCK FORMAT

99 Willow Street
Brooklyn, New York 11201
September 15, 19__

Phillips, McCann, and Frost Associates
33 Wall Street
New York, New York 10003

Attention: Personnel Department

Gentlemen:

On September 1 I sent to you an application and attached
resume for entry into your training program in the Securities
Trading market.

I hope that you are still considering my application. This training program is of great interest to me. I believe that my
experience in the business world qualifies me for a position
in your program, and that I would be a valuable asset to
your firm.

Thank you for your consideration. I hope to hear from you soon
as to the status of my application.

Sincerely,

Roberta Dearing

7.9 LETTERS CHECKING REFERENCES AND MAKING RECOMMENDATIONS

Modern business operates on a system of personal contact through the mail, by telephone, and in face-to-face meetings of individuals. In doing business, it sometimes becomes necessary to determine the credibility of a person or firm through its contact with other people and companies. When considering a job application or an application for credit or a loan, the information available from other people as to the applicant's character, ability, and suitability is of key importance in your decisions. Requests for information about an individual are called letters checking references; responses to these inquiries are called letters of recommendation.

Letters Checking References

A request for information on an individual should be specific and brief. You should name the person whose reference you are contacting, and you should describe the position applied for (or other reason making a reference request necessary). State how you come to be contacting the firm or the individual for a reference—either as a former employer or as a personal reference for an applicant.

In your letter, state exactly what kind of information you seek. A reference can include personal information or professional opinions on an individual. It is useful to let the reader of the letter know in what capacity you wish to employ the applicant; a recommendation can provide those valuable insights into an applicant's capabilities and work habits which a written application or a lengthy personal interview may not disclose.

Finally, let the reader know that all information provided to you will be kept confidential. Knowing this may make it easier for the person who writes a recommendation to be honest and open in his or her opinions.

Compose effective letters checking references using the Simplified Letter Planner in section 7.1 and the Contents Planner below. Be sure to express your appreciation for the reader's help in each of these letters. Read the sample letter and use it as a guide for your own writing.

CONTENTS PLANNER—LETTERS CHECKING REFERENCES

The person who I need information on is:

He/She is applying for:

The duties of the job or requirements for acceptance (as in the ability to pay back a loan) are:

I am contacting the reader because the applicant is associated with him/her in the following manner:

The specific information I need on the applicant is as follows:

LETTER CHECKING A REFERENCE—FULL BLOCK FORMAT

COMMERCIAL PAPER COMPANY　　　　　　*Paper for All Purposes*

115 Mariposa Street
Denver, Colorado 80223

January 10, 19__

Alabama Paper Incorporated
45 Southern Parkway
Mobile, Alabama 36607

Attention:　Personnel Director

Gentlemen:

We are currently considering Mr. Harold Laser for the position of assistant research chemist with our company.　This position requires extensive familiarity with the development of specialty commercial papers.　As the most recent employer listed on his application, we are contacting you for information concerning Mr. Laser.

We would appreciate your opinion of Mr. Laser's performance during his employment with your firm, and your feelings about his suitability for filling the position we have available. Character, creativity, and the ability to handle important decisions are all important considerations in our selection of an applicant for this job.

Of course, all information you furnish will be kept confidential. Thank you for your help.

Sincerely,

Carole Lombardo - Personnel Manager

LETTER OF RECOMMENDATION—SIMPLIFIED FORMAT

Alabama Paper Incorporated
45 SOUTHERN PARKWAY
MOBILE, ALABAMA 36607

January 20, 19__

Ms. Carole Lombardo - Personnel Manager
Commercial Paper Company
115 Mariposa Street
Denver, Colorado 80223

HAROLD LASER

Ms. Lombardo, it is my pleasure to recommend Mr. Harold Laser

for the position of assistant research chemist with the

Commercial Paper Company.

Alabama Paper has employed Mr. Laser for ten years. During that

period he worked in our Development program in various capaci-

ties, finally as an assistant research technician. At all times

he excelled, efficiently, creatively, and thoroughly perform-

ing all the activities necessary to his position. We feel that

Mr. Laser is very suitable for any job available in his field

of expertise.

Mr. Laser has proven himself an honest and dedicated individual.

His record of community service and as a respected father will

make him not only an asset to your organization, but to your

city as well.

NELSON R. REDDING - PERSONNEL DIRECTOR

Letters of Recommendation

An answer to a request for information on an individual should attempt to fulfill the request as closely as possible. Name the individual about whom you are writing at the beginning of the letter, and the position (or other matter) for which you are recommending him or her. Be honest in your answers to the specific questions asked in the letter checking the reference, and courteous to the reader and to the applicant.

Writing letters of recommendation can be a delicate art. Remember that your reference can be the determining factor in the decision of another person or firm. Stress the favorable qualities of the person about whom you are writing. Praise the traits which you feel would be most valuable to a prospective employer or creditor. Shortcomings of a personal or professional nature need not be mentioned if they would have little bearing on the applicant's suitability for employment or credit. Be as considerate as possible to the subject of a letter of recommendation, but above all be truthful and honest. Your response to a letter checking a reference is always kept confidential.

Compose effective letters of recommendation using the Simplified Letter Planner in section 7.1 and the Contents Planner below. Read the sample letter and use it as a guide for your writing.

CONTENTS PLANNER—LETTERS OF RECOMMENDATION

The person I am recommending is:

He/She is applying for:

I know or employed him/her in the following capacity:

I have known him/her for the following length of time:

My personal opinion of the applicant's character is:

My opinion of the applicant's professional qualities is:

I believe the applicant can be an asset (or good credit risk) for the following reasons:

My opinion of the applicant's future promise is:

8

TECHNICAL MATTERS IN BUSINESS WRITING

8.1 ENVELOPE AND PAPER CHOICE

Most paper used in business correspondence is called *rag bond*. This paper has a high content of long fibers, which gives the paper surface a smooth and attractive grain. In addition, this paper has a *basis weight* of at least 20 pounds. This heavy stock ensures long life and good handling and correcting qualities. *Air mail* stationery is lighter in weight in order to save on higher overseas postage charges. Most air mail stationery has a basis weight of 13 pounds.

Continuing sheets and envelopes must match letterhead in color, finish, weight, and quality. Most businesses will order a complete complement of blank sheets and envelopes when ordering letterhead stationery.

Business-reply cards used in sales letters, order letters, and some general correspondence are usually specially printed on heavy card blanks.

Each common size for business stationery includes a specific paper size and matching envelope. These envelopes are either called *regular* if of the normal type or *window* if the front of the envelope has a clear plastic-covered opening for the inside address enclosed on the letter. *Double-window* envelopes have two separate windows for both the address and the return address enclosed on the form inserted in that envelope. Window and double-window envelopes are primarily intended for the mailing of special forms like receipts, invoices, and special message-reply forms.

Below is a list of the sizes of stationery and their corresponding envelopes. Use corresponding paper and envelope sizes in order to attain the most attractive appearance for your business correspondence.

STATIONERY AND ENVELOPES

STATIONERY	SIZE	ENVELOPE	SIZE
Standard	8½″ x 11″ or 8½″ x 10½″	No. 9, No. 10, No. 6¾	3⅞″ x 8⅞″ 4⅛″ x 9½″ 3⅝″ x 6½″
Executive or Monarch	7¼″ x 10½″ 7½″ x 10″	No. 7 or Executive	3⅞″ x 7½″
Half-Sheet or Baronial	5½″ x 8½″	No. 6¾ or Baronial	3⅝″ x 6½″

8.2 *ADDRESSING THE ENVELOPE*

The following information must appear on all envelopes used for business correspondence: the address, the return address, the special mailing and on-arrival notations, the attention line, and any other special handling notation necessary for proper delivery.

The *address* should be placed just below the centerline of the envelope, slightly to the right of center. Use the same format as used in the inside address, but insert the *attention line* used on the letter between the addressee's name and the mailing address. If the special notation *Care of* or *c/o* is necessary for delivery, also insert this notation between the addressee's name and the mailing address.

The *return address* is placed in the upper left-hand corner of the envelope. If letterhead stationery is used, envelopes should be provided with return addresses already printed. When you use plain envelopes, type your name and address, single-spaced internally, as it would appear in the inside address of a letter addressed to you.

Special mailing notations, if used, are typed directly below and to the left of the stamp. All notations should be completely capitalized. If a letter is to be sent via air mail, a special air mail sticker can be used if the air mail envelope does not bear the designation already.

On-arrival notations like PERSONAL or CONFIDENTIAL are typed completely capitalized three or four lines below the return address, close to the left edge of the envelope.

Special handling notations needed for the proper delivery of the letter (such as *Please Forward, Hold for Arrival,* or *Will Pick Up*) should be typed in upper- and lower-case, underlined, and positioned in the lower left-hand corner of the envelope.

Sample Layout for Business Envelopes

```
RETURN ADDRESS
                                                    STAMP
ON-ARRIVAL NOTATION
                              SPECIAL MAILING NOTATION




                        xxx  ADDRESS   xxx
                        xxxxxxxxxxxxxxxxx
                        xxxxxxxxxxxxxxxxx
                        xxxxxxxxxxxxxxxxx




Special Handling
```

8.3 FOLDING AND INSERTING THE LETTER

When you have correctly matched the size of the envelope to the size of the stationery, folding the letter attractively and inserting it easily into the envelope is a simple chore.

1. For *standard-size letters* in *No. 9 or No. 10* envelopes; *executive or monarch size* in *No. 7* envelopes; *half-sheet or baronial* in *No. 6¾* envelopes:

Place the complete letter, pages in order, on your desk face up. Fold the lower third of all the pages together up over the message. Then fold the upper third of all the pages together down to meet the folded edge of the pages. Insert the letter so that the final fold faces the closed bottom of the envelope.

2. For *standard-size letters* in *No. 9 or No. 10 window* envelopes; *8½" x 11" special forms* in *No. 9 or No. 10 window* envelopes:

Place the complete letter or form, pages in order, on your desk face up. Fold the top third of the letter *back* so that the inside address and return address are in correct position for the envelope window(s). Then fold the bottom third of all the pages together up over the message so that the bottom edge of all the pages meets the folded edge of the pages. Insert the folded sheet so that all necessary information is visible through the envelope window(s).

3. For *standard-size letters* in *No. 6¾* envelopes; *8½" x 11" special forms* in *No. 6¾* envelopes:

Place the complete letter or form, pages in order, on your desk face up. Fold the bottom of the letter up so that the edge of this bottom section falls ½" below the top edge of the pages. Then fold the right third of the letter over onto the folded pages. Finally, fold the left third of the letter over the folded right third so that the left edge of all the pages is aligned with the previous fold. Insert the folded letter so that the final fold faces the closed bottom of the envelope.

8.4 PUNCTUATION

Punctuation helps you control your writing. Proper use of the various punctuation marks will make your sentences clear to readers. This section is a guide to the accepted punctuation practices in modern writing. Its alphabetical arrangement will help you locate and effectively use punctuation marks in your business correspondence.

Apostrophe (')

1. Is used with the letter *s* to form the possessive form of singular common and proper nouns and indefinite pronouns;

Robert's book   the boy's pencil   anyone's game

Note that possessive personal pronouns (*his, hers, its, ours, theirs,* and *yours*) do not take an apostrophe because they are already in the possessive form.

2. Is used to form the possessive form of plural nouns:

   the girls' overcoats   their mothers' homes   the men's hats

Note that when a plural noun ends in *s*, the apostrophe is used after the *s* to form the possessive form. If a plural noun does not end in *s*, *'s* is added to form the possessive form.

3. Is often used with *s* to form the plural of numbers, and the plural of words or letters used as words:

   6's and 10's   I used too many *but's*.   Be sure to dot your *i's*.

4. Is used to mark the omission of a letter or letters in a contraction and to mark the omission of numerals in certain numbers:

   aren't   I'm   couldn't   in the winter of '47

5. Is used alone and with *s* in expressions of measurement, money, or time:

   twenty dollars' worth   a week's vacation   a mile's drive

Brackets ([]) (always used in pairs)

1. Are used to set off editorial comments (material not written by the original author) in quotations:

   "The walls [in the bedroom] had crumbled."

2. Can be used to set off material within material enclosed in parentheses:

   Lehrmann, *Colors* (Chapter 4 [and other sections])

Colon (:)

1. Is used to punctuate a formal greeting, like the salutation in a business letter with mixed or closed punctuation:

   Ladies and Gentlemen: Dear Ms. Riley:

2. Is used to introduce a series or list:

   We have many items: meats, produce, dry goods, and dairy products.

3. Is used to introduce an explanation or example:

   Keeping warm in winter depends on one simple rule: the more you eat, the better you feel.

4. Is used to introduce a lengthy formal quotation, usually indented and not enclosed in quotation marks:

   That idea is best expressed in the opening lines of Lincoln's *Gettysburg Address:*

5. Is used to direct the readers' attention to a word or phrase:

   The prospectors had found the greatest prize: gold.

6. Is used to punctuate special headings in correspondence:

SUBJECT: Attention: Enc.:   STO:anf

7. Is used to separate a title from a subtitle:

Modern Automobiles: Using New Materials and Technology

8. Is used in expressions of time and to separate elements in a bibliographic listing:

2:15 P.M.   Chicago: New Education Publishing, Inc.

9. Is used to indicate a relationship between elements such as a ratio:

100:1   a:b   persons:seats

Comma (,)

1. Is used to separate clauses in a sentence:

To remedy this situation, we should call the electrician.
I wanted to speak to you, so I came to your office.

2. Is used to separate words or phrases in a series:

We have cats, dogs, and birds.
He wants free medical care for the elderly, a system of housing for the homeless, and equal taxes for the rich and the poor.

3. Is used to set off an interjection or an interrupting element within a sentence:

We might, despite overwhelming odds, win this game.
Standard Aluminum, the largest producer of special alloys, will not raise its prices.

4. Is used to set off contrasting elements within a sentence:

Automobiles, not motorcycles, are supposed to park here.
The more they hear, the more they will tell.

5. Is used to separate multiple adjectives that describe the same noun:

It was an old, noisy, creaky car.

6. Is used to set off an introductory, interruptive, or closing phrase that is part of a quotation:

"We saw that dog again," Sally said.
"If you use our tools," the salesman said, "you will find your work much easier."

Note that the comma falls *within* the quotation marks if it is used in this manner.

7. Is used to set off words used in sentences to directly address a person or thing:

We sent your order out yesterday, Mr. Helms, so it should arrive soon.

8. Is used to indicate omitted words in an elliptical clause:

Richard bought a jacket; Phillip, a pair of boots.

9. Is used to avoid confusion or ambiguity by separating words within a sentence:

> Mr. Fargo, our personnel supervisor Ms. Wood will call you.
> Besides tires, cars need other replacement parts.

10. Is used to punctuate dates in traditional forms:

> April 15, 19 ___

Inverted date forms are unpunctuated:

> 15 April 19 ___

If the day of the month is omitted, the comma between month and year is optional:

> . . . in April 19 ___ . . . *or* . . . in April, 19 ___ . . .

11. Is used to punctuate addresses, both in inside addresses and in textual references to addresses:

> Ms. Ronnie Calano
> 15 Grace Court
> Brooklyn, New York 11201
>
> . . . when we were visiting Burlington, Vermont . . .
> . . . who lives at 375 Dean Street, Denver, Colorado . . .

12. Is used to punctuate complimentary closings in letters using mixed or closed punctuation:

> Sincerely yours,   Very truly yours,

13. Is used to separate numerals of more than three digits into easily readable forms:

> 7,345,222

In numerals of four digits, the comma is optional:

> 3,890 *or* 3890

14. Is used to punctuate names written in inverted form:

> Harding, Eleanor P.

15. Is used to set off elements within a commercial name and to set off a title at the end of a personal name:

> Sealing Collection Agency, Inc.
> Harvey O. Tucker, M.D.
> Ralph A. Rennet, Vice-President

16. Is used to punctuate the salutation in personal correspondence:

> My dearest Greg,   Dear Sandra,

Dash (—)

1. Is occasionally used to set off a word or phrase for emphasis:

> The reasons—both public and private—affecting our decision are complex.

The directors were shocked—completely shocked—to hear of your resignation.

2. Can be used to indicate an abrupt break in thought or logic:

We have many items available—but I am sure none would interest you.

3. Can be used to separate the summarizing clause from the main part of the sentence:

Tables, sofas, chairs, and mirrors—these were the pieces stolen from our warehouse.

4. Can be used to clarify sentences including interjections punctuated with exclamation points or question marks:

The house you bought—was it in Nevada?—seems like a valuable investment.

Ellipsis Points (. . . or . . . .)

1. Are used to indicate a word or words omitted from the middle of a quotation. Three periods (. . .) are used in this case:

"Automobiles are often trouble-free but . . . are often known to cause great problems."

2. Are used to indicate a word or words omitted at the end of a sentence. Four periods (. . . .) are used in this case:

The books were in the aisles, on the shelves, and in the sorting bins. . . .

3. Can be used in written dialogue to represent a pause or an incomplete sentence:

"Audrey said . . . I mean Charlie said . . . well, actually it really wasn't. . . ."

Exclamation Point (!)

1. Is used to terminate a command or an especially emphatic phrase, sentence, or interjection:

Look at that!   Send us your order—right now!

2. Can be used to convey the writer's surprise:

The President (!) called to wish him a happy birthday.

Hyphen (-)

1. Is used to show where a word that must be divided at the end of a printed line should be divided:

The subject of this correspondence is the delivery of
your merchandise.

2. Is used in certain compound nouns:

    a cover-up   assistant-principal   U-turn

3. Is used to separate parts of a compound adjective used before the noun it describes:

    baby-faced boy   weak-kneed attitude   over-aged cheese

4. Is used in certain compound verbs:

    hog-tie   stir-fry   blow-dry

5. Is used in a compound fraction or number when it is written out:

    one-quarter pound   two-hundred thirty-three

6. Is used in certain words to separate the prefix from the main part of the word:

    vice-treasurer   semi-sweet   ex-director

7. Can be used to represent the words *to, between,* or *up to and including,* indicating a relationship between two separate elements:

    Rome-New York flight   the Mets-Cardinals game

Parentheses ( ) (always used in pairs)

1. Are used to enclose supplementary material in a sentence:

Robert Donnely (age 38) was admitted into the hospital today.
In Verona (Italy) today, it was ten degrees below zero.

2. Are used to enclose directions to the reader in a sentence:

The most popular item in our stock is the least expensive (see Fig. 1).

3. Are used to enclose numerals confirming a written-out number:

one-thousand (1000) pen-and-pencil sets
three hundred dollars ($300.00)

4. Are used to enclose numbers or letters that mark items in a list or series:

We sent you this model because (1) we were out of the model you ordered, (2) that model has been discontinued, and (3) this new model is the equivalent of the one you ordered.

5. Are used to enclose the abbreviation of a written-out term:

The American Automobile Association (AAA) is a well-known group.

Note that end-of-sentence punctuation marks occur after the closing parenthesis *unless* the parentheses contain a complete sentence:

We placed the data in an easy-to-read chart (see page 2).
We placed the data in an easy-to-read chart. (See page 2 for the complete chart.)

Period (.)

1. Is used to terminate an imperative or declarative sentence, and some sentence fragments:

> Bring your books home.   The cow was in the barn.
> Send in the order form. Right away.

2. Is used to follow initials and punctuate certain abbreviations:

> Ms. I. J. Dewey   Dr. J. C. Hart   p. 18   col. 7
> Allan Dobbs, Sr.   Jack Lowery, M.D.   3:15 P.M.

3. Is used to follow a number or letter symbol standing alone in a list or an outline:

> Our customers are:
> 1. Companies
> 2. Private individuals
> 3. Charitable organizations
>
> I. How the election works
>   A. Primary nominations
>   B. The primary election
> II. Selecting the candidates
> 4. Is used to mark decimals in numerals:

> 35.998 $10.50

Question Mark (?)

1. Is used to terminate an interrogative sentence (question):

> How are you?   Is the merchandise I ordered on the way?
> Can you (1) send a replacement or (2) give a refund?

2. Can be used in a sentence or in lists to indicate the writer's uncertainty:

> David Jones, the mayor's assistant (?), came in today.
> Jonathan B. Carpenter, 1567– ?

Double Quotation Marks (" ")

1. Are used to enclose a quotation or a fragment of quoted matter when it is reproduced exactly as it was first stated:

> "The letter was a great success," he said.
> " . . . ask what you can do for your country."—John F. Kennedy

2. Are used to enclose special words or phrases borrowed from others, or to introduce special words or terms:

> As they say, Kentucky Fried Chicken is "finger lickin' good."
> These "yahoos" were exactly like those Swift talked about in *Gulliver's Travels.*

3. Are used to enclose the titles of:

articles in magazines	short stories
chapters of books	songs
catalogs	short musical compositions
lectures	radio and television episodes
short poems	

Note that titles of books and magazines are italicized (underlined), rather than enclosed in quotation marks.

4. Rules for use of other punctuation marks when double quotation marks are used:

The closing double quotation mark always follows a period or a comma:

"We were present at the meeting," said the vice-treasurer, "but we still do not remember that discussion."

The closing double quotation mark always comes before a colon or semicolon:

The class had completed T. S. Eliot's poem "The Love Song of J. Alfred Prufrock"; this was the first time many students had read a modern American poet.

The closing double quotation mark comes before a dash, exclamation point, or question mark when it refers to the entire sentence:

Did she ask about "our dear mother"?
Was it Carol who said "the hat is so ugly"?

The closing double quotation mark comes after a dash, exclamation point, or question mark when it refers only to the matter enclosed In the quotation marks:

Mr. Roberts asked, "Why did you close the lid?"
"I can't leave you now!" yelled Harry Converse.

When both single and double quotation marks are used in a sentence, the period at the end of the sentence generally falls within *both* the closing single and the closing double quotation marks.

Single Quotation Marks (' ')

Are used to enclose a quotation within a quotation:

Mr. MacIlhenny said, "I remember when my mother used to say 'Don't get your feet wet.'"

Semicolon (;)

1. Is used to join main clauses not linked by a coordinate conjunction (such as *and, but,* or *or*):

United Chemicals is a well-known company; they have subsidiaries all over the world.

2. Is used to join main clauses joined by *transitional connectives* (such as *also, then,* or *thus*):

> Our class has read the poetry written by American authors in the early twentieth century; thus we can be prepared to discuss the cultural attitudes of that period.

3. Is used to present a list or series separate from the main part of a sentence when the list is introduced by an appropriate expression:

> Great mathematicians often play musical instruments; for example, Einstein played the violin, and Newton the harpsichord.

4. Is used to separate items or clauses containing other internal punctuation:

> We have offices in Billings, Montana; San Francisco, California; and Tokyo, Japan.

Virgule (/)

1. Is used to represent *or* when it presents alternatives:

His / hers outerwear

2. Is used to represent *per* in expressions of volume, speed, or distance:

25 gal / min   500 ft / sec

3. Is used to represent *and* or *to* in certain shorthand notations:

in the block of 45 / 46 street
during the fiscal year 19—/—

4. Is used as a punctuation mark in certain abbreviations:

p / l statement   C / D

5. Can serve as a divider between lines of poetry quoted in the text of a prose document:

> . . . In bower and hall / He wants them all / Nor can dispense / With Persia for his audience . . .
>
> —Emerson

8.5 CAPITALIZATION

While there are no hard and fast rules dictating capitalization procedures in modern business correspondence, there are certain standard conventions followed by most businesses and individuals. Use these rules and the preferences of your organization to capitalize correctly within your own writing.

1. Capitalize people's names and titles referring to specific individuals:

Ronald Reagan   Mr. President
Mr. Abbott   the Chief Justice
Uncle Harry

2. Capitalize nationalities, organizations, and references to the members of each:

> German   a German woman
> The Lions Club   a Lion

3. Capitalize all geographic entities (places):

> Germany   North America   the Red River
> the Brooklyn Bridge   the West   South Street

Do not capitalize the points of the compass:
> south   north   east   west

4. Capitalize names of religions and religious groups:

> Christianity   the Unitarian Church

5. Capitalize names of the Deity and pronouns referring to the Deity:

> God   the Holy Ghost   Him   His

6. Capitalize the personal pronoun *I:*

> You and I should become friends.

7. Capitalize days of the week, months, special days, and generally known historic events:

> Sunday   September   Easter   the Crusades

Do not capitalize the names of the seasons:

> winter   spring   summer   fall

8. Capitalize all trade names:

> Kleenex   Bazooka bubble gum   Coca-Cola

9. Capitalize terms using derivatives of names, places, and nationalities if that derivative is clearly associated with the original name, place, or nationality:

> French literature   New York cheesecake   Swiss chocolate

10. Capitalize the name of a school subject if the name is a proper noun or the name is followed by a numeral:

> Physics 101   Italian

11. Capitalize the first word of a sentence, sentence fragment, direct quotation, or line of poetry:

> Send in your application! Immediately!
> "I don't think so," said Aunt Mabel, "the potatoes were very good without any butter."
> I strolled across/ An open field/ The sun was out/ Heat was happy . . .
> —Theodore Roethke

12. Capitalize all words in titles except articles *(a, an, the)*, coordinate conjunctions *(and, or, but)*, and prepositions of less than five letters *(of, in, by)*; if the coordinate conjunction, article, or preposition is the first word of the title, it must be capitalized:

> *The Writer's Handbook* (book)
> "A Poem is a Walk" (short poem)

The Man of LaMancha (musical composition)
"You and Me Against the World" (song)
Chief Justice of the Supreme Court (person)
The President of the United States (person)

13. Capitalize words used as headings for charts, tables, and lists when they are followed by a numeral:

Figure 5   Fig. 5   Number 25295   No. 25295

14. Capitalize terms of common personification (terms referring to inanimate objects as persons):

Mother Nature   The Angel of Death   Jack Frost

8.6 ITALICIZATION (UNDERLINING)

Italicization (the equivalent in typed or handwritten material is underlining) is a method of separation or differentiation of certain words or phrases used in sentences. These rules are a summary of the accepted uses of italics.

1. Italicize titles of books, periodicals, lengthy poems and musical compositions, and motion pictures:

The Catcher in the Rye (book)   *Newsweek* (magazine)
The Waste Land (long poem)   Beethoven's *Ninth Symphony*
Star Wars (motion picture)

2. Italicize the names of ships, trains, aircraft, and spacecraft:

the *Queen Mary* (ship)   the *Orient Express* (train)
The Enola Gay (airplane)   *Explorer III* (spacecraft)

3. Italicize to specially emphasize a short phrase or word within a sentence:

If you want to save money, *send in this form immediately*.
The train was approaching *fast.*

4. Italicize to indicate words, letters, and figures used as words:

He forgot the word *and* in the sentence.
Wilbur always dots his *i*'s and crosses his *t*'s.
The most difficult numeral for children to write is *8.*

5. Italicize to indicate words considered foreign when used in normal business English:

The history of that country is a story of *noblesse oblige*.
This area is commonly known as *el barrio*.

6. Italicize statements of court cases in their traditional or contracted forms:

Smith v. *Star Security*   the *Smith* case   *Smith*

8.7 RULES FOR WORD DIVISION

Neat, effective presentation of typed correspondence is an important quality of good writing. In order to give typed or printed text a uniform appearance with even margins, you will occasionally have to divide (hyphenate) long words which would seriously intrude upon your page margin. Sometimes, moving a long word to the following line in order to prevent the run-over into the margin is all that is necessary. But that option may cause an unsightly gap at the end of the previous line. In cases such as these, dividing the word between two lines is the only option.

Since so much time has been devoted to determining a clear method of word division by so many different writers, it is not strange that there are many sets of rules explaining different word division procedures. In general, any good modern dictionary will be useful in determining the correct place (or places, in the case of certain words) to divide a word between two lines. But whatever source of information you choose, there are some common sense rules for word division that will save you time and bother.

1. If there is space for a hyphen at the end of a typed line, there is room for one or two letters needed to complete a word. Similarly, if you need to divide a word between lines in order to avoid a one- or two-character gap at the end of a line, move the entire word to the next line. That gap will be insignificant.

Avoid divisions like: af-   un-   a-
                    ter   fit   piece

and: epidem-   orega-
          ic   no

2. To avoid confusion among readers, divide compound words linked with one or more hyphens at the hyphen:

vice-   face-to-   person-   beach-
chairman   face   to-person   comber

If absolutely necessary, divide compound words linked with one or more hyphens in another place:

vice-chair-   per-
man   son-to-person

3. Divide closed compounds (compounds linked without a hyphen) between main elements:

window-   radio-   hover-   over-
pane   telephone   craft   throw

Try to avoid dividing closed compounds in another place:

win-   radiotele-
dowpane   phone

4. Avoid dividing dates and addresses between lines. If necessary, divide a date or address *only* at the comma within:

April 15,   Barrington,
19 ___   Rhode Island

Do not divide the address on an envelope or in an inside address.

5. You may separate the long preceding title from an individual's name if space is tight in an inside address or on an envelope:

The Honorable   The Most Reverend
Thomas Ciccone   Daniel Mahoney

Do not divide either the name or the title internally.

There are certain times when words should not be divided between lines. Follow these rules whenever possible:

1. Do not divide the last word on a page.
2. Do not divide the last word of a paragraph.
3. Names, courtesy titles, and degrees or titles following names should not be divided in addresses or bodies of letters.
4. Abbreviations of all kinds should not be divided between lines.
5. Numerals and units of time, money, distance, or other measurement should not be divided between lines.

8.8 CONTRACTIONS

Contractions (shortened forms of common words) are not used in formal business writing. Since you will have to write spoken dialogue as it occurs, and write social and personal letters, knowledge of contractions is necessary because they are used in these writing styles.

The apostrophe (') is used to denote omitted letters in contractions. When constructing contractions using the following rules, insert the apostrophe in the exact place where you have omitted letters.

Contractions with Pronoun Stems

These stems are pronouns:

I   you   he   she   it   that
they   these those what   who   we

1. When the pronoun stem is used with *am, are,* or *is* to make a contraction:

    CONTRACTION = stem + *'m, 're,* or *'s* (appropriate word minus first letter)
    examples: *I'm, you're, he's*

2. When the pronoun stem is used with *have* or *has* to make a contraction:

    CONTRACTION = stem + *'ve* or *'s* (appropriate word minus first two letters)
    examples: *I've, you've, he's*

3. When the pronoun stem is used with *shall* or *will* to make a contraction:

    CONTRACTION = stem + *'ll*
    examples: *I'll, you'll, she'll*

4. When the pronoun stem is used with *had, should*, or *would* to make a contraction:

> CONTRACTION = stem + *'d*
> examples: *I'd, you'd, she'd*

Negative Contractions with Verb Stems

These stems are forms of verbs:

are	can	could	did	do	does	had	has
have	is	must	need	should	was	would	

When the verb stem is used with *not* to form a common contraction:

> CONTRACTION = stem + *n't*
> examples: *aren't, didn't, hasn't*

Exceptions: Do not use *ain't* in the place of *am not*.
> *Will not* is contracted as *won't*.

Special Contractions

1. Long words

   association—ass'n   *temporary—temp'y*

2. Multiple words

   where is—where's   *of the clock—o'clock*

3. Years

   1960—'60

The omitted numeral, letter, or word is replaced by an apostrophe in all of these special cases.

8.9 COMMON SYMBOLS

Monetary Units

$	dollar(s)
¢	cent(s)
£	pound(s)
/	shilling(s)
F	franc(s)
¥	yen

Mathematical

+	plus
−	minus
±	plus or minus
×	multiplied by
·	multiplied by
÷ or /	divided by, fractional notation
=	equal to
≠	is not equal to
≡	identical with
≈	is approximately equal to
>	greater than
<	less than
≥	greater than or equal to
≤	less than or equal to
∫	integral
∂	derivative
√	square root
:	is to (in ratio)
::	as (in complex ratio)
∴	therefore
∵	because
Δ	changes or change in
∝	varies as
0	zero
∞	infinity
‖	parallel or parallel to
∠ or ⋨	angle
∟	right angle
⊥	perpendicular to
△	triangle
▭	rectangle
▱	parallelogram
○	circle
⌒	arc of a circle
π	pi

Astronomical

☉	the Sun
⊕, ⊖, or ♁	The Earth
●	new moon
☽	first quarter
☾	last quarter
○	full moon

Medical

℞	take
℥	ounce
ʒ	dram

Other Symbols

@	at
&	and
*	asterisk
°	degree
%	percent
′ ″	feet and inches, minutes and seconds (on maps)
#	number, pounds
©	copyright
®	registered trademark
a/c	account of, air conditioned
♂	male
♀	female
→	yields, produces; or flows toward
{	brace—represents a grouping
"	ditto marks
ç	cedilla—*c* pronounced as *s:* français
ö	dieresis—second vowel pronounced separately: coördinate
é	acute accent
è	grave accent
∧	caret—indicates an insertion
√	check
¶	new paragraph
☠	poison

8.10 ABBREVIATIONS

United States Postal Service Abbreviations

The following is a list of unpunctuated two-letter abbreviations recommended by the United States Postal Service for use with ZIP codes. These abbreviations replace the abbreviations common to older business correspondence:

Alabama	AL	Connecticut	CT
Alaska	AK	Delaware	DE
Arizona	AZ	Florida	FL
Arkansas	AR	Georgia	GA
California	CA	Hawaii	HI
Colorado	CO	Idaho	ID

Illinois	IL	Ohio	OH
Indiana	IN	Oklahoma	OK
Iowa	IA	Oregon	OR
Kansas	KS	Pennsylvania	PA
Kentucky	KY	Rhode Island	RI
Louisiana	LA	South Carolina	SC
Maine	ME	South Dakota	SD
Maryland	MD	Tennessee	TN
Massachusetts	MA	Texas	TX
Michigan	MI	Utah	UT
Minnesota	MN	Vermont	VT
Mississippi	MS	Virginia	VA
Missouri	MO	Washington	WA
Montana	MT	West Virginia	WV
Nebraska	NB	Wisconsin	WI
Nevada	NV	Wyoming	WY
New Hampshire	NH	District of Columbia	DC
New Jersey	NJ	Canal Zone	CZ
New Mexico	NM	Guam	GU
New York	NY	Puerto Rico	PR
North Carolina	NC	Virgin Islands	VI
North Dakota	ND		

Other Abbreviations

Any good, modern dictionary will help you determine correct forms for common abbreviations. In general, follow these rules for the use of abbreviations:

1. You may abbreviate *titles preceding names:*

   Mr., Messrs., Dr.

2. You may abbreviate a title if you use the *complete name* or *first initials of a person's name and surname:*

   Col. Robert Ryan   Col. R. Ryan   *but*   Colonel Ryan

3. You may abbreviate *titles following names:*

   Kevin Dodge, M.D.   Allen Parsels, Sr.

4. You may abbreviate *terms used repeatedly in a written document.* When the term first appears, write it out in full and follow it with its appropriate abbreviation enclosed in parentheses. After that, you may use only the abbreviation.

5. You may abbreviate certain *terms with numerals.* Do not use that abbreviation without the numeral:

   See Chap. 3.   *but*   See the following chapter.

6. You should abbreviate *proper nouns* with *capital letters;* other words should be abbreviated with lower-case letters:

   U.N.   U.S.A.   *but*   rpm   exec.   gal.

7. You may abbreviate most *governmental organizations and common company names* with capital letters not divided by periods:

NRC   DoD   CBS   IBM

8. Certain abbreviations are already plural in form. To make other abbreviations plural, simply add an *s* after the singular form of the abbreviation (within the closing period, if one is present):

assns.   Figs. 2 and 3   Chaps. 9 and 10   lbs.

8.11 TERMS AND EXPRESSIONS TO AVOID

Effective business correspondence is clear and concise. Unfortunately, trite and overused expressions have developed which are confusing, static in spirit, or redundant. Since these expressions often fall in very visible sections of business letters, such as introductions, closing paragraphs, and complimentary closings, a single hackneyed phrase can damage the impact of an entire letter. Thus avoiding these words and expressions is an important job for successful correspondents.

These expressions fall into three categories: long and unnecessarily involved expressions; stiff, antiquated words and phrases; and redundant statements or phrases. It is impossible to individually list all of the mistakes writers make in correspondence; but if you are aware of these general categories of mistakes and the simple ways to correct them, then your writing will be fresh, original, and clear.

1. *Long, involved locutions* such as "we will institute the necessary inquiries" can always be pared down to simple, clear, basic phrases like "we will inquire" or "we will try to find out." Use these shorter expressions in your writing. Omit all unnecessary words when trying to say something you want your readers to understand.

2. *Old, stilted, and unnecessarily formal expressions* such as "beg your indulgence" or "Thanking you in advance, I remain," have modern, less formal equivalents. Use "ask" or "I would appreciate . . ." and other short, modern, and less trite phrases in your writing.

3. *Redundant (repetitive) phrases* which have come to be common parts of corporate English have no place in letters written by successful correspondents. Look out for phrases such as "please forward on this letter to . . ." and "we would like to repeat again . . ." Trim the extra word or words away from your central meaning. Do not pad your sentences with additional words; emphasis comes from clarity, not repetition.

Use the following list of some of the most common avoidable expressions to guide your own writing. While all of the phrases that are outmoded, wordy, or redundant are not included, this list will serve to show how you can give your writing an original and contemporary spirit.

Overly Wordy Expressions

Expression	Use instead
abovementioned item	this item
	that item
	the item
above, the above,	as we have said
as stated above	see (page or section)
acknowledge receipt of	(have) received
affix (one's) signature	sign
aforementioned item	this item
aforesaid item	that item
	the item
	(name of item)
at about (time)	at (time)
	about (time)
at all times	always
at an early date	soon
	immediately
	by (exact date)
at this point in time	now
at this writing	presently
at your earliest convenience	soon
	immediately
	by (date)
brought to our notice	we note
	we see
	we notice that
letter dated (date)	letter of (date)
	(date) letter
despite the fact that	though
	although
	even though
due to the fact that	because
	since
duly (action)	(action)
(as in duly appreciated)	(appreciated)
earnest attempt	attempt
earnest endeavor	try hard
endeavor	try
	make every effort to
for the purpose of	for
have before me	omit and rewrite
(like: I have before me your bill of January 25.)	(according to your January 25 bill)

in the amount of	for (amount)
in the amount for	
in the course of	during
in the event that	if
	in case
in view of	because
in view of the fact that	since
be in a position to	can
be within (one's) power to	are able to
prepared to offer	can offer
	offer
reason is because	because
	The reason is (reason)
	the reason is that
recent date	recent (item)
of recent date	(item) of (date)
return mail	immediately
	at once
subsequent to	following
	after
take the liberty of (action)	are (action)
(like: take the liberty of sending you these pamphlets)	(are sending you these pamphlets)

Overused and Antiquated Expressions

Expression	Use instead
advise you that	say that
	tell you that
as per	as
as to	regarding
	concerning
	about
as regards	regarding
	concerning
assuring you that	you can be sure that
	you can be certain that
attached hereto	attached is/are
attached herewith	here is/are
beg	omit
beg to (expression)	use the expression alone
enclosed please find	enclosed is/are
	here is/are
esteemed (as in	omit
esteemed presence)	(your presence, your arrival)
favor	your letter, check, order, etc.
as in your favor of [date]	(your letter of [date])
hoping to hear from you,	I/we look forward to hearing from you.
hoping for the favor of a reply, I/we	I/we look forward to your reply.
remain,	(modern complimentary closing)

in re	concerning
meet with (one's) approval	is acceptable to (name)
	is approved by (one)
oblige	omit and rewrite
(like oblige us with a reply)	(please reply)
of the opinion that	believes that
	thinks that
party	the person
(like the party who called earlier)	the individual
	(the person who called earlier)
pending receipt of	until we receive
prior to	before
pursuant to	concerning
	according to
	following up on
receipt is acknowledged	we have received
same	it
(like we have received same)	them
thanking you in advance, I remain,	I will be grateful for your help.
	Any help will be appreciated.
	(modern complimentary closing)
therefor	for
therein	inside
thereon	on
thereto	to
trusting you will	I hope you will
	I hope you can
undersigned	I
	me

Redundant phrases

Expression	Use instead
advised and informed	told
	let him/her know about
and etc.	etc.
raise to a maximum	increase
	maximize
reduce to a minimum	lessen
	minimize
refer back	refer to
	look back at

INDEX

Italicized numbers indicate illustrations.